Presented to: Justine

By: Debbie

Date: Jan. 25, 2022

Congratulations!

Happy Birthday
to a great friend and
a wonderful mom!

What a *Great Word*

FOR MOMS

ALSO BY KAREN MOORE

What a *Great* *Word*

FOR MOMS

A DEVOTIONAL

KAREN MOORE

Faith *Words*

NEW YORK   NASHVILLE

FaithWords
Hachette Book Group
1290 Avenue of the Americas, New York, NY 10104
faithwords.com
twitter.com/faithwords

First Edition: April 2019

FaithWords is a division of Hachette Book Group, Inc. The FaithWords name and logo are trademarks of Hachette Book Group, Inc.

The publisher is not responsible for websites (or their content) that are not owned by the publisher.

The Hachette Speakers Bureau provides a wide range of authors for speaking events. To find out more, go to www.hachettespeakersbureau.com or call (866) 376-6591.

ISBNs: 978-1-5460-3564-0 (paper over board), 978-1-5460-3563-3 (ebook)

Printed in the United States of America

LSC-C

10 9 8 7 6 5 4 3 2 1

Contents

GOD'S PROMISES

CAN YOU HELP ME?

You Are an Awesome Mom!

"Many women do noble things, but you surpass them all."

Proverbs 31:29 NIV

Chances are that you seldom reflect on all the amazing things you do for your family. You're the first one to show up with a warm hug or a listening ear and tender heart to help divert a crisis. You're the one who never misses a beat between caring for your household and doing those things you were designed to do just for yourself. The truth is, there's really no one quite like you.

This little book was written to inspire your thoughts as you grow and move forward from here. Each word is genuinely directed toward aligning your work, your spiritual growth, and your hopes and dreams as you are molded and shaped into the person God intends you to be.

As you meditate on, contemplate, or consider each word, it might help to create a journal for the forty words you see here and then notice how your perceptions of these special words change with time and experience. Make each word personal to you. Let it motivate your heart and inspire your spirit.

Since you are the family counselor, cook, and caretaker, you need the full armor of God to face each day. No worries! He knows you, sees you, and is ready to walk with you wherever you go.

It's exciting to see the things that God will do through you, and through the wisdom and kindness and guidance you've given your children. You make a difference to your family, your friends, and all who have the privilege to know you.

Once a mom, always a mom! May God bless you and keep you. You are a gift of love to your family.

In His Love,
Karen Moore

Train Your Children in the Way They Should Go

When children are given encouragement, they learn to believe in themselves.

When children are treated with kindness, they learn the Golden Rule.

When children are rewarded for their efforts, they learn to appreciate and value what they've done.

When children receive approval, they learn to trust themselves.

When children are given recognition, they learn that success takes hard work.

When children are treated with respect, they learn to honor others in return.

When children are surrounded by love, they learn to be givers as well as receivers.

When children are given a foundation of faith, they learn to walk with God.

K. Moore

Woman

There's No One Quite Like You

Charm is deceptive, and beauty is fleeting;
*but a **woman** who fears the LORD is to be praised.*
Honor her for all that her hands have done.   Proverbs 31:30–31 NIV

You have a lot of roles to play as a mom, and you take on each one with everything you've got. You create, orchestrate, remind, nourish, and encourage each person in your family in ways that serve them well. It's a big job, and some days, it makes you downright weary!

Since you are a woman with a great heart who puts God first, God knew you would be a remarkable mother. He knew that you would have the courage to turn to Him when you had doubts or questions. He knew you would do your best to be a faithful mother, friend, and prayer warrior. You wear a lot of hats, and you wear each of them well.

One of the reasons you are honored by those around you is that the cornerstone of your life is built on faith. Your faith is what helped you become the woman you are today, one who is respected by friends and peers, one who is a blessing and fun to be around. You deserve praise for all you do for your family. You are always learning more about what it means to be a woman with a heart for God.

There's no one quite like you! It's no wonder God put you in the exact place you are in today. He knew you would do your best to guide with love and patience. He knew your reverence for Him would shine through in all you do as a mom.

As you continue to open your heart to God, He will draw near, embracing you as His beloved child and causing you to grow. No matter what comes your way, you can be sure that God will stand by you through all the days ahead. Thanks for being such a remarkable woman of grace and love.

YOU HAVE WHAT IT TAKES

Because I am a woman, I must make unusual efforts to succeed.
If I fail, no one will say, "She doesn't have what it takes."
They will say, "Women don't have what it takes."

Clare Boothe Luce

INSPIRING WOMEN

Women, we need you to give us back our faith in humanity.

Desmond Tutu

WHAT YOU DO SO WELL

Accustom yourself continually to make many acts of love, for they
rekindle and melt the soul. Teresa of Ávila

YOU KNOW WHAT IT MEANS TO LOVE

This is the miracle that happens every time to those who really
love:

The more they give, the more they possess. Rainer Maria Rilke

YOUR FAITH AND LOVE

A Christian should always remember that the value of good works
is not based on the number and the excellence, but on the love of
God which prompts the doing of those good things!

John of the Cross

A WOMAN OF WORTH

You are a woman after God's own heart,
The gift of His love; a Divine work of art.
He's known you and loved you
From the day of your birth,
You're a woman of God; a woman of worth! K. Moore

MOMISM

Nobody loves you like I do!

Mom's Prayer and Blessing

Dear Lord, I thank You for designing my life so that I could find You and establish a relationship with You. Ever since we first met, I've been trying to put together all the pieces of what I understand in Your Word, and what I sense from our prayer times together. You've sustained me, helping me grow past the times when I'm sure I disappointed You, and loving me into being the woman I am today.

You've blessed me in ways too numerous to count, watched over my family and the people I love in this world, and helped me to become stronger both as a woman and as a mom. You've been my Source of renewal and grace. I pray that You will continue to walk with me all the days of my life, for I don't want to go anywhere without You! Amen

Attitude

You Are Positively Radiant!

You were taught, with regard to your former way of life, to put off your old self, which is being corrupted by its deceitful desires; to be made new in the attitude of your minds; and to put on the new self, created to be like God in true righteousness and holiness.   Ephesians 4:22–24 NIV

You've always had a certain flair, a kind of radiance that makes everyone smile when you enter a room. It's part of what makes you special to those close to you. Your family and friends appreciate how well you let your light shine with a positive attitude, and an approach to each day that announces, "I can do it. I am ready to face the world!"

Of course, you know it wasn't always this way. Your radiant spirit is part of the gift God gave you as you've learned to walk with Him through your daily life. Everything changed the day you surrendered your life to His grace and mercy. He renewed you and helped you develop a new attitude of love and patience. Your friendship with the God of your heart now filters through everything you do. It is built around an attitude, a mindset, a decision to turn your life over to God because surrender brings hope, and results in joy.

Your amazing example inspires your children to be the best they can be because you look for the best in them, trusting in God to watch over them, and believing that they will become thoughtful and generous adults. You share your heart and your faith, instilling confidence and giving them a sense of real worth and security.

You're a "can do" mom, who looks forward to all that can be, never looking back to what was, but looking for the brightest stars in the sky, listening to the voice of your Savior, praying to draw closer to His side. Your attitude of joy, of praise, of love for God radiates through your home and out to all who know you. Thanks for all you do to let your light shine.

WHEN YOU'RE A MOTHER

Being a mother means that your heart is no longer yours.
It wanders wherever your children do.   George Bernard Shaw

BECAUSE MOMS FIND THE SILVER LINING

"It's snowing still," said Eeyore gloomily.
"So it is."
"And it's freezing."
"Is it?"
"Yes," said Eeyore. "However," he said, brightening up a little, "we haven't had an earthquake lately."   A. A. Milne

MOM'S GOOD WORKS

She must be known for her good works—works such as raising her children, welcoming strangers, washing the feet of God's people, helping those in trouble, and giving her life to do all kinds of good deeds.   1 Timothy 5:10 NCV

MOM'S ATTITUDE

To look up and not down,
to look forward and not back,
to look out and not in,
and to lend a hand.   Edward Everett Hale

POSITIVELY MOM!

It is no use to grumble and complain,
It's just as cheap and easy to rejoice;
When God sorts out the weather and sends rain—
Why, rain is my choice!   James Whitcomb Riley

MOMISM

There's no use crying over spilt milk!

Mom's Prayer and Blessing

Dear Lord, I thank You for blessing me with such an amazing family. It's not always easy to do the job of being a mom, but I wouldn't trade it for anything. I think I manage to do it with a positive attitude and a good spirit most days, and I know that attitude comes from You. You have guided me and listened to me when I needed help. You have seen me when my nerves are all on edge and my patience is low, and have boosted me up, and helped me to stay strong and keep everything in perspective.

I pray that when I feel overwhelmed by frustrating events or when the kids are unwilling to cooperate with me, You would bless me again with the kind of attitude that stays positive, speaks with love, and handles each situation gently. In all that You do for me, Lord, I can have nothing but an attitude of gratitude. Bless each member of my family today. Amen

Change

Change, It's the Only Constant in Life!

*And he said: "Truly I tell you, unless you **change** and become like little children, you will never enter the kingdom of heaven."*   Matthew 18:3 NIV

Most of us don't really appreciate change. We work hard and get our lives into a place that is comfortable and predictable, and the last thing we want is to have our lives change. The problem is that human beings and life are dynamic, and nothing ever stays the same. In truth, we need change to stimulate our growth and keep us moving forward.

It's interesting that our God, Who is unchanging—Who is the same yesterday and today and forever—wants us to change; at least He wants us to grow and become more of what He dreamed we might be. Change is the great constant, and the more we embrace it, or even initiate it, the more we feel fulfilled by the work we do—the more we understand that we are making progress.

As a parent, you witness the continual changes that your child goes through from the totally dependent, fragile person that you brought home from the hospital, to the one who first took a stand and toddled across the living room floor, to the college graduate, ready to step out into the world. Kids are all about change, all about the variables that make life interesting and challenging.

One of the things that doesn't have to change though is your childlike faith. What this means is that your faith isn't modified by becoming an adult. It is faith that still trusts in the hand of God to be there. It's faith that knows God can do anything and that all things are possible with Him. It's faith that runs to God during a crisis and seeks His embrace, and His advice and favor.

Keep your childlike faith as you grow through all the phases of your life, as a woman, as a mom, and as a faithful servant of the Lord. God is with you through every change you will ever experience, ready to help you if it seems overwhelming, ready to comfort you if it contains sorrow, and ready to move you forward as you understand more of what He has for you. Change is not to be feared or dreaded. It is to be embraced and anticipated, especially when you realize that you're the daughter of the King and that He wants only your best.

May you be blessed with amazing changes in your life, fulfilling your dreams and answering your prayers.

MAKING PROGRESS

We all like progress; we just don't like change.

Author unknown

HOW TO MAKE A CHANGE

1. Start immediately.
2. Do it with outrageous enthusiasm.
3. No exceptions.

William James

MOM'S INFLUENCE

Never doubt that a small group of thoughtful, committed people can change the world. Indeed, it is the only thing that ever has!

Margaret Mead

CHANGE A HABIT

Good habits are hard to acquire, but easy to live with.
Bad habits are easy to acquire, but hard to live with.

Zig Ziglar

MY, HOW YOU'VE CHANGED!

Do the things that show you really have changed your hearts and lives. And don't think you can say to yourselves, "Abraham is our father." I tell you that God could make children for Abraham from these rocks.

Matthew 3:8–9 NCV

DON'T GET TOO COMFORTABLE

If you would attain to what you are not yet, you must always be displeased by what you are. For where you are pleased with yourself, there you have remained. Keep adding, keep walking, and keep advancing.

Saint Augustine

MOMISM

Change your underwear: You never know when you might get into an accident!

Mom's Prayer and Blessing

Dear Father in Heaven, I usually like gradual change, the kind that doesn't upset the daily routine or make me move too far past my comfort zone. I don't like surprises and I never like changes that happen suddenly, when I have no choice, but to accept the new normal that it brings.

I'm so grateful that You never change, Lord, and that I can depend on You to be there when I need You, and that You will help me walk with You in childlike faith. It's not always easy, but I know with Your help, I can do it.

Forgive me when I resist the kinds of changes You want to make in my life. Help me to embrace all that You have for me as we walk together through the next few months and years. Thank You for blessing my family through all the changes we have made and for sticking with me as I grow and become the woman you designed me to be. Amen

Choose

It Pays to Be Choosy!

*You did not **choose** me, but I chose you and appointed you so that you might go and bear fruit—fruit that will last—and so that whatever you ask in my name the Father will give you.*   John 15:16 NIV

You may remember a peanut butter commercial that said, "Choosy mothers choose Jif!" The point of the ad was to remind you how awesome you are because you know how to make brilliant choices, at least when it comes to choosing peanut butter. As a mom, your abilities span way beyond peanut butter as you make myriad choices every single day.

You've been choosing what to do since you first began a family. You made a choice whether to work outside your home or whether to work from home, or you may have chosen whether to homeschool your kids, or whether to send them to public or private school. You choose the best you can based on all the information you have available to you.

God wants you to be a choosy mother. He wants you to be wise and discerning, looking to Him for help when you're not certain just how to choose. He knows you and He knows what is best for your family. The first thing He wants, of course, is for you to choose Him right back. As you see in this Scripture, initially you didn't choose Him; He chose you. However, since He chose you, He has desired a great relationship with you, and that means you have to choose Him, not just once, but every single day. With God's help, you can choose confidently and wisely. When you choose to stay close to Him through daily prayer and Bible reading, He can help you even more.

The reason God chose you in the first place is that He trusts you to plant every seed of love He provides and let it bear fruit in the hearts of each member of your family. He knew you would stand strong in your faith and make great choices in the ways you parent and live your life. Choosy mothers choose God!

CHOOSE LIFE

Now choose life, so that you and your children may live and that you may love the Lord your God, listen to his voice, and hold fast to him.   Deuteronomy 30: 19–20 NIV

YOU CAN ALWAYS MAKE A NEW CHOICE

Every moment you have a choice, regardless of what has happened before.

Choose right now to move forward positively and confidently into your incredible future.   Author unknown

BECOMING YOURSELF

Every time you make a choice, you are turning the central part of you, the part that chooses, into something a little different from what it was before.   C. S. Lewis

OUR GREATEST CHOICE

The decision we all face is this: Whether to consciously lock God out of our lives or open the door of our heart and invite Jesus Christ to come in.   Luis Palau Jr.

WHY? BECAUSE I SAID SO!

Yes and No are the two most important words that you will ever say.

These are the two words that determine your destiny in life.
                                                        Author unknown

GO AHEAD, MOM, CHOOSE!

In any moment of decision the best thing you can do is the right thing.

The next best thing you can do is the wrong thing.

And the worst thing you can do is nothing.   Theodore Roosevelt

CHOOSE WHOM YOU WILL SERVE

"But if serving the LORD seems undesirable to you, then choose for yourselves this day whom you will serve, whether the gods your ancestors served beyond the Euphrates, or the gods of the Amorites, in whose land you are living. But as for me and my household, we will serve the LORD."

Joshua 24:15 NIV

MOMISM

I'm doing this for your own good!

Mom's Prayer and Blessing

Dear Lord, I am so grateful that You chose to be in my life and that I chose you right back. I know that I haven't always shown You how much that means to me, but I hope to walk with You all my life. As I make choices for my family, Lord, help me to be wise and loving in the things I choose for them. Help me to listen to You and listen to their desires as well. It's not always easy to know what to choose, especially if I'm having to make a choice where I have no control over their situation.

I'm learning that being a mother means I simply must make choices, and then keep praying, leaving the results of those choices in Your hands. You have already taught me that You are there, and I can trust You to watch over the people I love so much. I raise my children up to You and thank You for choosing to be their Heavenly Father, and I pray that they would then choose You right back. Amen

Effort

Nobody Does It Like You, Mom!

*For this very reason, make every **effort** to add to your faith goodness; and to goodness, knowledge; and to knowledge, self-control; and to self-control, perseverance; and to perseverance, godliness; and to godliness, mutual affection; and to mutual affection, love.* 2 Peter 1:5–7 NIV

Every mom has gifts that others can easily identify. You can probably think of those things your own mom did that were simply her. You didn't really know anyone else who could bake a pie, or soothe a hurt, or tell a great story like she could. Moms have a unique kind of character and personality, and most kids figure out how to use those special traits to their advantage. They are gifted at knowing how to flatter Mom to get on her good side so that she agrees to whatever they're asking for.

Your parenting effort changes with time, though, because you're always learning and gaining new insights as you grow with your kids. After all, no one really gave you a rule book for the different phases of child rearing, so you've had to keep learning how to manage everything. You do this because you want your efforts to pay off. You want to raise amazing children, shaping them into healthy adults and loving human beings. It's not an easy task at best, but God knew what He was doing when He put the family you have into your hands. He knew also that He would be right there with you to guide you all your life.

As a mom, you've learned to rely on your faith. That means you believe that your efforts are blessed, and that if you persevere and keep trying, the end results will be good for everyone around you. The most deliberate effort you make is to love. No matter what is going on, what moment of chaos may be happening in your house, you keep it in mind that the best efforts, the greatest challenges, must be handled with love. It is with that thought in mind, you have assurance that faith and love will serve you well.

Whatever you do today to love and guide your family, may God bless the work of your heart and your hands. He is with you always, blessing every effort you make.

MAKE THE EFFORT

Take a method and try it. If it fails, admit it frankly, and try another.

But by all means, try something.   Franklin Delano Roosevelt

A GREAT EFFORT

Work hard and cheerfully at whatever you do, as though you were working for the Lord rather than for people.

Colossians 3:23 NIV

GROWTH AND EFFORT

All growth depends upon activity. There is no development physically or intellectually without effort, and effort means work. Work is not a curse; it is the prerogative of intelligence, the only means to adulthood, and the measure of civilization.

Calvin Coolidge

EDUCATING MOMS

Though motherhood is the most important of all the professions—requiring more knowledge than any other department in human affairs—there was no attention given to preparation for this office.

Elizabeth Cady Stanton

MOM'S EFFORTS

It is better to build strong children than to repair broken men.

Frederick Douglass

HOW TO RAISE CHILDREN

Before I got married, I had six theories about bringing up children. Now I have six children and no theories.

John Wilmot, Earl of Rochester

Keep trying! Put your best foot forward!

Mom's Prayer and Blessing

Dear Father in Heaven, I can't imagine all the efforts You have made on behalf of human beings. No doubt, we've been stubborn children and have not made your job easy. When I think of all You've done, I want to do better, try harder, and do more to ensure that my family is well loved and well disciplined. You are my inspiration and my best example. You love us so much that You keep patiently trying to give us time to discover more of what we should do to be better children, better people. That alone helps me have more patience with my own family.

Today, I pray for all moms who make the effort to love their families and to serve You. I pray that You would bless them and watch over them, protecting them from any harm and showering them with Your amazing grace and love. Help all those who watch over children to be able to keep doing their jobs well. Bless moms and grandmothers and teachers and childcare workers everywhere today.

Amen

Love

Mom Is Another Word for Love

Love is more important than anything else. It is what ties everything completely together.
Colossians 3:14 CEV

Nothing makes life worthwhile like love! Love causes us to rejoice in the good that comes our way and helps us celebrate wonderful events and milestones in the lives of our children. Love brought each of your children into the world, hugging them through the ups and downs of grade school, listening to the frustrations they experienced through high school, and sending them with a bit of sadness from the nest when they finally emerged as healthy and happy adults, ready to go out into the world. Love is what moms do best because it's the biggest part of every motivation of their hearts.

You are the first gift of love your child ever receives. You are the best definition of what it means to be loved and to feel loved. You know what love is because you invited Jesus to come into your heart. Divine love shapes your heart and your attitudes in ways that can help you be an amazing mom. Divine love steps in when your patience is running short, or your frustrations are getting the best of you. Divine love reminds you what it means to forgive and to begin again with each new day.

God's love shows you that nothing could ever come between you, nothing could ever separate you from the ones you love, and nothing could keep you from loving unconditionally. Mothers who love like that inspire their children to become all they were meant to become.

That's what you do, Mom! You inspire an attitude toward forgiveness and kindness because you lead by example. Today, you can share your heart, speak gently and patiently, give your children room to grow. You can provide an environment of safety and thoughtfulness. You're a loving example and you serve your family with your whole heart. Love is the gift you bring to each new day. Well done, Mom!

THE GOAL OF LOVE

Love is the fulfillment of all our works. There is the goal; that is why we run. We run towards it and once we reach it, in it we shall find rest.

Saint Augustine

WHY GOD LOVES YOU, MOM

God loves you not because of who you are, but because of who He is!

Author unknown

MOM'S LOVE OVERFLOWS

May the Lord make your love increase and overflow for each other and for everyone else, just as ours does for you.

1 Thessalonians 3:12 NIV

WHAT MOMS KNOW

Love does not dominate; it cultivates! Johann Wolfgang von Goethe

THIS IS THE WAY MOMS LOVE

Love feels no burden, thinks nothing of trouble,
    attempts what is above its strength, pleads no excuse of
impossibility;
    for it thinks all things lawful for itself, and all things possible!

Thomas à Kempis

LOVE IS A HUG

Love is always open arms. With arms open you allow love to come and go as it will, freely, for it'll do so anyway. If you close your arms about love, you'll find you are left holding only yourself.

Leo Buscaglia

MOMISM

Love makes the world go 'round!

Mom's Prayer and Blessing

Dear Lord, You know how much I love my children and my family. Nothing in this world matters to me as much as they do, apart from my relationship with You. I pray that You will continually watch over all of us, helping us to love each other in ways that reflect Your love for us. Help us when we are in irritable moods or when we're weighed down by individual troubles, that as a family we can get through anything and that love is our greatest asset.

I pray, Lord, for all moms who seek to love You and to shine a light of goodness and blessing on their families. I pray for strength when we are worn out, kindness when our nerves are on edge, and patience when we simply don't think we have more to give. Life is not always easy, and parents don't always know what to do, but you know all about that since you are our Heavenly Parent. I pray to be an example of Your grace and love to my own family and to people who are part of my life wherever I may be. Thank You for being the steadfast Source of love for everyone who knows You. Your love makes all the difference. Amen

Kindness

Mom Is the Living Expression of God's Kindness

*God said to Moses, "I will show **kindness** to anyone to whom I want to show*
kindness, and I will show mercy to anyone to whom I want to show mercy."
Romans 9:15 NCV

Mother Teresa, that woman who probably had more compassion for others than any other person we might think of, had this to say about kindness: "Spread love everywhere you go. First of all, in your own house. Let no one ever come to you without leaving better and happier. Be the living expression of God's kindness: kindness in your face, kindness in your eyes, kindness in your smile, kindness in your warm greeting."

This message from Mother Teresa sets a high bar. There are days when it's all you can do simply to stay calm, much less overflow with kindness. It's not easy to be a mom, and sometimes it's a struggle. Those are the days when you probably long for someone just to be kind to you.

In your heart, you know you are a kind person. You can make others feel appreciated and genuinely cared about. You can offer your radiant smile and be a blessing. You can spread kindness wherever you go and you often do.

Nothing about kindness can be overrated. In a world in which we often fall short when offering compassion to one another, you can be an example and a beacon of light. You can bring a breath of fresh air to your family and friends simply by being kindhearted.

Kindness is what you can offer in your mothering, and to your friends and family. You can help others feel that life is okay and that things are getting better all the time. Sometimes you can do it by simply offering your smile and your expressions of warmth.

As you step into each day, may God bless your life with His gentle spirit. May He use you as an ambassador of good will because of your kind heart and your desire to please Him. You can always serve as a wonderful example of what it means to be a kind and compassionate woman and a thoughtful mom. Thank you for being wonderful you!

MOM'S SMILE

A warm smile is the universal language of kindness.

William Arthur Ward

CHILDREN NEED KINDNESS

The greatest thing a person can do for her Heavenly Father is to be kind to some of His other children.

Henry Drummond

GOD'S KINDNESS

But I show kindness to thousands who love me and obey my commands.

Exodus 20:6 NCV

MOM'S KIND HEART

A kind heart is a fountain of gladness, making everything in its vicinity freshen into smiles.

Washington Irving

THE WORK OF KINDNESS

Constant kindness can accomplish much. As the sun makes ice melt, kindness causes misunderstanding, mistrust, and hostility to evaporate.

Albert Schweitzer

MOM'S KIND WORDS

Sometimes she simply nods,
Or a smile lights her face,
But there's something special mom does
That nothing can replace.
She gently speaks with kindness,
And always does her part
To bless each special moment
With the love that fills her heart.

K. Moore

You will always be my baby!

Mom's Prayer and Blessing

Dear Lord, I so want to be a mom who is kind all the time; not just sometimes when I'm in the right mood, but all the time, offering a gentle word of encouragement. Lord, You know me well enough to see that I don't always achieve that goal. You know how I am! I can get off track quickly, imagine the worst before I come around and embrace the best, and even assume that I am somehow to blame for nearly all the troubles I hear about. I pray that You would keep me honest and help me to be a kinder, more patient, a more giving mom than I feel like I am.

Help me to make You proud of the way I treat my family, and when I slip, help me to do better. Kindness sounds like an easy idea, but I know that it is not all that simple to achieve. Thank You for loving me enough to help me become the kindhearted woman I truly want to be. Amen

Wonders

You Are a Mom Who Does Wonders

*Many, L*ORD *my God, are the **wonders** you have done, the things you planned for us. None can compare with you; were I to speak and tell of your deeds, they would be too many to declare.*   Psalm 40:5 NIV

You probably don't make a list of all the things you do for your family on any given day. Chances are that if you did, you would sit back in wonder, trying to imagine how you accomplished all those things. You take it all in stride, knowing that you are doing your best to keep things running smoothly. Your amazing attention to detail that keeps everybody happy is just part of the wonder of you.

If your children sent you a thank-you note today, they'd likely say something that resembles the Psalm noted here. They'd probably remind you that you have done amazing things for them since the day they were born. You planned for them in ways that nurtured their first steps and their first words. You made sure they went to good schools and you noted their skills and talents, helping them to get even better at the things they could do naturally. If they tried to make a list of all your good deeds on their behalf, they would discover there are too many to count.

You love knowing that your kids are well taken care of and that you've done all you can to help them grow. God feels the same way about you, His special daughter. He's been planning good things for your life since the day you were born. He has done wonders with you, and He knows you have done wonders with your family. He affirms you always with His own kinds of love notes, providing for your needs, shining a Light on your path, watching over your household.

May God continue to pour out His grace on your loving heart as you grow in understanding of all He has for you. He knows the gifts, talents, and blessings you bring to your family. The fact is, He knows you are wonder-full!

LESSONS FROM MOM

The mother's heart is the child's schoolroom.

Henry Ward Beecher

MY FAVORITE TEACHER

You have omitted to mention the greatest of my teachers—my mother!

Winston Churchill

MOM'S SUCCESS

She has achieved success who has loved much, laughed often, and been an inspiration to little children.

Adapted from Bessie A. Stanley

A GOOD DAY

Don't judge each day by the harvest you reap but by the seeds that you plant.

Robert Louis Stevenson

THE WONDERS OF GOD

Whatever it is that keeps the finer faculties of the mind awake, and the interest above mere eating and drinking, money-making and money-saving;

Whatever it is that gives gladness, or sorrow, or hope, be it violin, pencil, pen...

is simply a divine gift of Holy influence for the salvation of that being to whom it comes, for the lifting of a person out of the mire and up on the rock.

George MacDonald

WHEN GOD DOES WONDERS

God does **wonders** that cannot be understood; he does so many miracles they cannot be counted.

Job 5:9 NCV

MOMISM

You can't judge a book by its cover!

Mom's Prayer and Blessing

Dear Lord, I thank You for giving me time and energy and good health so that I can do my best for my family. Some days, I confess I wonder how I got into this family; I look at each person and part of me sees them as miraculous while part of me wonders what I was thinking when I signed up with all of them. Of course, You know I love each of them more than words can say.

You knew all along we'd make a great family. You knew our hearts and what we would need to get along with each other. You helped us learn how far we could stretch and bend and keep going without getting broken. You've brought a certain light to our hearts that keeps us aware of Your hand at work in our daily lives. It's amazing to me each time I stop to really reflect on what You've done. May I do little wonders for my family that in some way reflect the many wonders You have done for me. You are simply beyond awesome!   Amen

Giving

You're a Mom Who Always Gives from the Heart

Do not send me away from you or take your Holy Spirit away from me.
*Give me back the joy of your salvation. Keep me strong by **giving** me a*
willing spirit.   Psalm 51:11–12 NCV

Moms seldom think about what they give to their families. After all, they signed up to be a mom and giving is part of what makes it fun, and tiresome, and exciting, and disappointing, and delightful, and mysterious. Givers don't run out of ways to give because they always have one more resource—whether it's a prayer or a listening ear or a plate of brownies, they are there. Moms take giving as just part of the job description. They don't expect thanks or praise, even if they secretly wish someone would notice what they do.

Today, it's time to change all that. You are officially being recognized for all that you do, all that you give with no thought for yourself, simply because you love your family. You deserve a standing ovation, your name up in lights, and your lottery ticket to win the jackpot because of the generous person you are to everyone. Yes, it's your day to stand up and be counted.

Since you are used to giving beyond the call of duty, you may not even recognize the countless ways you bless your family. You have a generous and willing spirit, the kind that inspires those around you.

Because you give from the heart, you never seem to run out of the strength to give more. God has given you a portion of Himself, sustaining you with His love and kindness, a gift that everyone can see radiates from your soul, from head to toe.

Today, give yourself a break. Soak up the joy of being loved by your family, resting in the security that your Father in Heaven sees all that you do, and trusting that you are appreciated by each person who knows you. Thanks for being a precious and thoughtful giver, every day and in every way. You give "Motherhood" a good name! God bless you in all ways, for always.

WHAT MOMS BELIEVE

More blessings come from giving than from receiving.

Adapted from Acts 20:35

MOM'S CHEERFUL GIVING

A cheerful giver does not count the cost of giving.
The heart is set on pleasing and cheering on those to whom the gifts are given.

Julian of Norwich

WHAT MOMS ALREADY KNOW

Giving is the secret to a healthy life.
Not necessarily money, but whatever a person has of encouragement and sympathy and understanding.

John D. Rockefeller Jr.

ONE REASON MOM IS A GIVER

What mom can tell when some . . . fragmentary gift of knowledge or wisdom will enrich her children's lives? Or how a small seed of information passed from one generation to another may generate a new science, a new industry—A seed which neither the giver nor the receiver can truly evaluate at the time.

Helena Rubinstein

TAKE CARE OF YOURSELF, MOM!

Be yourself—truthfully.
Accept yourself—gracefully.
Value yourself—joyfully.
Forgive yourself—completely.
Treat yourself—generously.
Balance yourself—harmoniously.
Bless yourself—abundantly.
Trust yourself—confidently.

Love yourself—wholeheartedly.
Empower yourself—prayerfully.
Give yourself—enthusiastically.
Express yourself—radiantly.

Author unknown

MOMISM

It's better to give than to receive!

Mom's Prayer and Blessing

Dear Lord, I am so thankful that You have blessed me with the ability to have a generous spirit and a desire to give all that I can to my family. Nothing delights me more than having a chance to please them in special ways or surprise them with little gifts for no reason at all. I've learned from Your generous example that You keep giving to all of us even when we never stop to thank You. You give to us much more than we deserve through Your grace and mercy.

Help me to keep growing as a mom and as a giver so that I reflect the joy I feel simply because You are in my heart. Let me be an example of what it means to be an unconditional giver. Help me to be more like You!

Thank You for giving me such an amazing family. I pray for Your blessing and Your anointing over each of their lives. I thank You for all you give to me each day because I have learned that no one can out-give You!

Amen

Hope

Hope Is Always in Mom's Tool Kit

We also have joy with our troubles, because we know that these troubles
produce patience. And patience produces character, and character produces
hope. *And this hope will never disappoint us, because God has poured out*
his love to fill our hearts. He gave us his love through the Holy Spirit, whom
God has given to us.
Romans 5:3–5 NCV

Moms have troubles. They have struggles and disappointments as they raise their children. They wonder if they have enough influence over their children to make a difference, to see them straighten out their lives and become all that they are meant to be when things go awry. Moms experience heartbreak, but they never lose hope. They never stop believing in God's possibility for their children. They never give up.

How is that possible? It's possible for you because when you surrendered your life to Christ, you put all that you are and all that you have in His hands, including your children. When each child was born, you dedicated that child's life to Him, knowing that there might be times when you would need some divine intervention. The day you made that surrendered choice changed everything.

Why? You gave Jesus permission to walk with you and your child each day, sustaining life, and providing strength of mind and character. You blessed your children in ways they could not understand until they accepted the Light of Christ for themselves. You held them up in prayer, kept them in the Light, and offered wisdom and direction for their lives. You provided an atmosphere where mistakes could be made and be forgiven. Disappointments could occur and then be forgotten. Tears could be shed and then dried again with a smile. You are a mom who brings hope into every situation your family must face.

With your love and guidance, you have nurtured your family with real hope that helps them move out into the world. Thanks for always keeping hope alive and close to your heart!

MOMS ALWAYS HAVE HOPE

Faith means being sure of the things we hope for and knowing that something is real even if we do not see it.

Hebrews 11:1 NCV

WINGS OF HOPE

Hope is the thing with feathers
That perches in the soul,
And sings the tunes without the words,
And never stops at all.

Emily Dickinson

MOMS DO IT WITH HOPE

Everything that is done in the world is done by hope. No gardener would sow a grain of corn if he hoped not it would grow up and become seed. No tradesman would set himself to work if he did not hope to reap the benefits of his labors.

Martin Luther

MOM'S HOPE

If they can make penicillin out of moldy bread, they can surely make something out of you.

Muhammad Ali

MOMS HAVE HOPEFUL HEARTS

There's nothing like a little one
To make a mom feel blessed.
For from the start, her faithful heart
Helps her to do her best!

K. Moore

THE BASIS OF HOPE

Hope is not the conviction that something will turn out well, but the certainty that something makes sense, regardless of how it turns out.

Václav Havel

HOPE IS MOM'S WORD

The word which God has written into the heart of every mom is hope.

Author unknown

MOMISM

If you think you can do it, you can!

Mom's Prayer and Blessing

Dear Father, I have been growing in my faith for some time now and I have learned that I can trust You and put my hopes and dreams in Your confident hands for the well-being of each person in my family. I have hope because I know what You can do to change lives and breathe Your Spirit into your children. I am so grateful for all that You've shown me and all that You've done to let me know You are there for me.

I'm not always sure I've made the right decisions. Sometimes I feel too tired to know whether I've even adequately spent time with You seeking Your guidance and blessings. Help me to walk in continual hope, trusting that You know what is best for my children and my whole family. You alone know the purpose for which they were each born and so, Lord, I surrender them to Your care, hoping in You for all that they will become.

Amen

There's No One Quite Like Mom

———— ⁌ ————

Her children rise up and call her blessed.
Proverbs 31:28, NKJV

Some just call her Mama
The one who does her part
To make the boo-boos go away
With warm hugs from the heart.
Some will call her Mommy—
No matter what their age,
Knowing that she guided them
Through every growing stage.
For others she'll be Ma,
As she cooks and cleans and tries
To do her best to make life blessed
With a sparkle in her eyes.
Of course, for most, she'll just be Mom,
A curious kind of blend—
Of all that gives life meaning,
As she grows into a friend.
And finally, she'll be Mother,

Who worked, yet raised each one,
With courage, grace, and joy—
A job she'll never feel is done.
Yes, there's no one quite like Mother,
The one God picked to raise
The kind of loving children
Who will always give her praise.

K. Moore

Tenderhearted

Mom's Love Is Tied with Heartstrings

*And be kind to one another, **tenderhearted**, forgiving one another, even as God in Christ forgave you.*   Ephesians 4:32 NKJV

You may not feel this way all the time, but you were created with amazing heartstrings that attach themselves to those you love. Your tender heart is a gift from God, and it is an example of the kind of heart God has for His children. Your family benefits greatly from this quality in you, and God wants to help you become even more tenderhearted.

At times, your heartstrings can wrap themselves around others and bring them into your inner circle. When that happens, you treat everyone like family and give them your best self, your gentle spirit, and your kind words. These are not things people are used to getting out in the world and so they love to stand in your light; they love to be near you.

Perhaps you're thinking this description just couldn't be about you, but it is. Sure, you're still learning, but even when you're tired, you try to be kindhearted. After all, it is the Spirit of God within you that gives you that ability. You are His miraculous design and He helps you every day to have the energy and the desire to bless those around you.

Some imagine that tenderhearted people are not as strong, or as successful, as those who aren't willing to lead with their heart. You know what those people are like and you don't want to be like them. God is teaching you to see others through the eyes of love, through the light of God's love for them. That may well make you one of the strongest people on earth.

As a mom, you know all about what it means to be tough and tender. May your tender heart radiate to others today, affirming and encouraging them, and may it come back to rest on you as well, because God's heart is always tender toward you.

HEART EXERCISES

The best exercise for strengthening the heart is reaching down and lifting people up.

Ernest Blevins

STRENGTH AND GENTLENESS

Nothing is so strong as gentleness.
Nothing so gentle as real strength.

Saint Francis de Sales

A WORD TO THE WISE MOM

See that your primary focus is about your heart:
That there, God's image may be planted,
That there, God's interests may be advanced,
That there, the world and temptations are subdued,
That there, the love of sin is cast out,
That there, in your heart, the desire for holiness grows.

Adapted from Jonathan Edwards

GUARD YOUR HEART

Above all else, guard your heart, for everything you do flows from it.

Proverbs 4:23 NIV

A SOFT AND TENDER HEART

The heart must be kept tender and soft,
Open to God's inspiration and guidance,
Ready to speak His glory.

Author unknown

A HAPPY HEART

Where your pleasure is, there is your treasure;
Where your treasure is, there is your heart;
Where your heart is, there is your happiness.

Saint Augustine

MOMISM

I will love you till the cows come home!

Mom's Prayer and Blessing

Dear Lord, I believe that I am a woman with a soft heart. I do my best to offer a listening ear and gentle guidance to my family. I look for the best in each person and encourage their thoughts and actions. Of course, there are days when I tuck my tenderhearted side away because I feel too stressed or overwhelmed by other things in my life. When that happens, I don't deal with my family with the kind of compassion they deserve. I ask Your forgiveness for those times and pray that you would restore me to be more of what You want me to be... tender and strong. Thank You for teaching me to see people with the heart first, to look for the good in them, and to bring out the best in them. I'm certain I would not be that way all on my own.

I am grateful that when Jesus came into my heart, He swept away the things that could cause my heart to be hard or stubborn, and replaced them with a tenderness that I have embraced ever since. Help me to be faithful and strong, and always willing to show compassion to others, especially to my own family. Amen

Trust

Moms Build a Foundation of Trust

*But I am like a green olive tree in the house of God; I **trust** in the mercy of God forever and ever.*   Psalm 52:8 NKJV

One thing you do as a mom is to figure out who is trustworthy. The world is complex, and people are not always easy to read. It can be hard to tell the good guys from the bad guys. What's a mom to do?

If you put your trust in yourself, that's a good place to start, but it's not a good place to end. You're sure to let yourself down and get discouraged, losing confidence and trust. Trusting yourself, then, is a weak foundation.

If you put your trust in friends, that could be even trickier. After all, they will not always rise to the occasion when you most need them, and as life moves on, your friends will move with it. You're left again with a void, a feeling of uncertainty about who you can rely on, who will be there when you really need them.

If you put your trust in your work or your money, you're always aware that the job could be lost, or the money could suddenly be swept away. Falling stock prices or expenses you weren't counting on come out of nowhere. Money is not a good foundation.

God is the only One you can really trust. With Him, you won't have to worry about the good guys and the bad guys, and you won't have to wonder about His time or availability. He's always there for you. He's the Cornerstone for everything you need. Though we readily print "In God We Trust" on our money, we don't always recall the slogan when money issues dominate our thinking, or when our cash flow feels nonexistent. We discover that trusting God is a "no matter what else is happening" proposition.

Begin each day with God, the Cornerstone of all things, and He will open the way for you to stand forever on His strong foundation. You can trust in His mercy and goodness. That's His lifetime promise!

WHY MOMS TRUST GOD

In God alone there is faithfulness and faith in the trust that we may hold to Him, to His promise and to His guidance.

To hold to God is to rely on the fact that God is there for me, and to live in this certainty.

Karl Barth

I TRUST YOU, GOD!

I pray that the God who gives hope will fill you with much joy and peace while you trust in him. Then your hope will overflow by the power of the Holy Spirit.

Romans 15:13 NCV

MOM'S FAVORITE BOOKMARK

Let nothing disturb you, nothing frighten you;
All things are passing; God never changes.
Patient endurance attains all things;
Whoever possesses God lacks nothing;
God alone suffices.

Teresa of Ávila

A MOM'S LAMENT

I know God won't give me anything I can't handle.
I just wish He didn't trust me so much!

Mother Teresa

SLEEP TIGHT, MOM!

Have courage for the great sorrows of life and patience for the small ones;

And when you have laboriously accomplished your daily tasks, go to sleep in peace.

God is awake.

Victor Hugo

LASTING TRUST

Trust the past to God's mercy,
trust the present to His love;
and trust the future to His providence.

Saint Augustine

THE WORK OF MOTHERS

The very vastness of the work raises one's thoughts to God, as the only One by Whom it can be done—that is the solid comfort—He knows.

Florence Nightingale

IT'S OKAY TO BE A CLINGING VINE

Let us keep to Christ; and cling to Him; and hang on Him; so that no power can remove us.

Martin Luther

MOMISM

I've got eyes on the back of my head!

Mom's Prayer and Blessing

Dear Lord, I admit that I'm not always clinging to You as I should. When difficulties arise, I go into problem-solving mode, doing everything I can to figure out how to remedy the situation. Sure, I finally come to You in prayer, but more often than not, I'm just looking for You to affirm what I plan to do, rather than listening to what You would have me do. I know that is not a definition of trust.

Help me to trust You so much that I wouldn't think of making a move without You. I pray that trust will always remove doubt as I lean on Your faithfulness and your mercy. Keep walking with me, Lord, and bless my family. I lift them all up to You and trust that You will be with each one I love forever and ever.

Amen

Prayer

Without Mom, We Haven't Got a Prayer!

*Therefore confess your sins to each other and pray for each other so that you may be healed. The **prayer** of a righteous person is powerful and effective.*

James 5:16 NIV

Prayer is talking to God. You and God are in conversation and you both talk and listen. It's a nice exchange, and by the time you're finished praying, you feel better. You feel better because you took your concerns to the only Source who can actually do something about them. God is delighted because He just spent time with you, one of His greatest joys.

When you became a mom, it's likely you prayed regularly. Hardly a day passed that your children didn't cause you to think of something that you needed to take to God. As you've developed a more comfortable prayer life, you've learned a lot that you can pass on to your children, which helps them become people of prayer as well. One of the treasures of being a mom is that you can share stories of what God has done for you, and in turn, your kids will share stories about what God has done for them.

Some people concern themselves with the "how" of prayer. Should they say certain things or get into a specific posture for prayer? They wonder if they have the right words that will get God's attention and help them get answers from Him. But prayer is one of those things you simply can't do wrong. As long as you are talking to God straight from your heart, you are connected to Him and He is listening. If you are willing to listen in return, your prayer life grows more meaningful and comfortable.

It's important to pray for each member of your family, seeking God's guidance with questions and concerns, looking to Him for affirmation on the plans you make, and waiting to hear His voice as you go through the day. Your prayers may not change your situation right away, but they will change your heart, and they will remind you that you are never alone, because anytime you need to talk to God, He's right there with you. Your prayers are both powerful and effective as you pray for your children and for all the people you love.

Prayer is one of the greatest gifts God has given to us. He allows us to come right to the foot of the cross and lay down every concern of our hearts. Thank Him, praise Him, share your heart and mind and listen for His voice. It's that simple! You are a prayer warrior!

THE LORD'S PRAYER

Our Father in heaven, hallowed be Your name. Your kingdom come. Your will be done on earth as it is in heaven. Give us this day our daily bread. And forgive us our debts, as we forgive our debtors. And do not lead us into temptation, but deliver us from the evil one. For Yours is the kingdom and the power and the glory forever. Amen.   Matthew 6:9–13 NKJV

GIVE GOD A CALL

All who call on God in true faith, earnestly from the heart, will certainly be heard, and will receive what they have asked and desired, although not in the hour or in the measure, or the very thing which they ask; yet they will obtain something greater and more glorious than they had dared to ask.   Martin Luther

THE HEART OF PRAYER

When you can't put your prayers into words, God hears your heart.
                                                    Author unknown

HEAVEN'S ANSWERS

Heaven is full of answers to prayers for which no one ever bothered to ask.   Billy Graham

MOM'S PRAYER

It isn't always easy, Lord,
To face another day, to be the one in charge
Of all I do and say. So lift me up this morning, please,
And help me make a start at caring for my family
With a warm and loving heart. Amen

K. Moore

WORRIED?

Pray and let God worry!

Martin Luther

ASK, SEARCH, KNOCK

Ask and it will be given to you; seek and you will find; knock and
the door will be opened to you. For everyone who asks receives; the
one who seeks finds; and to the one who knocks, the door will be
opened.

Matthew 7:7–8 CEV

MOMISM

Without Mom, we haven't got a prayer!

Mom's Prayer and Blessing

*Dear Father in Heaven, I'm still learning what it means to come to You
in prayer. As a mom, I always seem to have something I need to put
before You. I thank You for my wonderful family and the opportunities
and challenges that they bring to my life. I thank You for trusting me to
raise my children well and for staying near me to guide and sustain me
in the process.*

*Some days, I'm not sure that I'm doing a very good job at being a
mom, but even on those days, I'm grateful to You for each hug and kiss
and smile I have a chance to share with my kids. You inspire my heart
to want to do a better job so that each person in my family thrives and
becomes all You designed them to be. Bless my home, Lord, and help me
to be the best mom I can possibly be.*

Amen

Teach

Moms Teach by Example

*Come, my children, listen to me; I will **teach** you the fear of the LORD.*
Psalm 34:11 NIV

You were the first teacher your children ever had. You showed them how to smile and rocked away their tears. You kept them warm and nourished their hearts and minds and bodies. You helped them begin life in the best possible ways.

Whether your children are still young, or whether your older children simply reflect on this idea, they will one day confirm that you were a great teacher. You gave them guidance as they took their first steps into the world. You helped them get back up when they fell, and you encouraged them to try, try again.

By your example, they learned that life requires patience and effort. By your love, they learned to become all that they could be.

The beauty of the teacher and the student dynamic is that each one teaches and each one learns. Your children taught you how to manage all that they had to deal with. They taught you to set boundaries so that they could thrive. They taught you to look on the bright side of life and not be quite so serious about things. You learned from them, and they developed skills and confidence because of you.

God has more to teach you as well as your life goes on. He gave you Jesus to be an example of what it means to trust Him with your whole heart and to go to Him when you need help with the challenges life brings. God gave you a positive spirit that takes on challenges and grows through them, taking each lesson and getting the benefit from it.

Thank you for teaching your children well and for doing all you can to shine a light on what it means to trust in God, listen to Him, and know that He watches over those who receive Him in love. He delights in you and He will continue to teach, bless, and guide your life from here to Heaven. May God bless you and keep you close to His heart today.

A GOOD THOUGHT FOR MOM

I never teach my pupils. I only attempt to provide the conditions in which they can learn.

Albert Einstein

IN PRAISE OF MOM

She taught me how to tie my shoes,
And how to brush my hair.
She taught me all the ABCs
And that it was good to share.
She told me words are special,
And it's important to be nice,
And before you say something mean
You really should think twice.
She told me all God's stories,
And about His only Son,
And she said that Jesus loves me,
No matter what I've done.
She built a strong foundation
That will last me all my days,
So any time I think of Mom,
My heart is filled with praise!

K. Moore

TEACHER'S REPORT CARD

The mediocre teacher tells.
The good teacher explains.
The superior teacher demonstrates.
The great teacher inspires.

William Arthur Ward

A LEARNER'S LAMENT

Personally, I'm always ready to learn, although I don't always like being taught.

Winston Churchill

ONCE A MOTHER, ALWAYS A MOTHER

No matter how old a mother is, she watches her middle-aged children for signs of improvement.   Florida Scott-Maxwell

MOM'S TRAINING

Train up a child in the way he should go,
And when he is old he will not depart from it.

Proverbs 22:6 NKJV

MOMISM

If you don't learn from your mistakes, there's no sense making them!

Mom's Prayer and Blessing

Dear Lord, I thank You for the opportunity that I have had to guide my children through each stage of life. I pray that I've done my job well and that it will please You to guide and direct me as I seek to help them grow further. Help me to learn with them, growing in my faith, developing greater understanding of what they really need from me. I know that it is a privilege to be a mother and I want to do all that I can to be a positive and loving influence.

I pray that Your kindness and favor will rest on my children all the days of their lives. Mold them and shape them into healthy, strong, and caring adults. Inspire me to share more of You with them as they grow, teaching them how beautiful it is to have a relationship with You, their Father and Creator. Bless their hearts and minds and keep them close to You always.   Amen

Patience

Lord, Give Me Patience, and Give It to Me Right Now!

*Therefore, as God's chosen people, holy and dearly loved, clothe yourselves with compassion, kindness, humility, gentleness and **patience**.*

Colossians 3:12 NIV

If you didn't have the opportunity to practice the limits of your patience before, you have probably learned more than you wanted to know since the day you became a mom. Kids require a lot of patience, because as soon as they run out of theirs, they are trying yours. Some days, you have all you can do to maintain the control it takes to calm everyone's nerves, including your own.

It's no wonder that we call patience a virtue. It requires fortitude and discipline, tolerance and gentleness of spirit. It's a big card to play. In Scripture, we refer to Job as a guy who had a lot of patience. He not only had to have patience to endure all the tragic events that were happening to him, he had to endure the criticisms of his friends, who seemed to think it was all Job's fault that life had taken a nasty turn. If you know the story, you know it wasn't Job's fault, but that didn't matter; he still had to listen to his friends talk on and on about what they thought his problems really were. Now that took patience!

As much as motherhood requires patience, keep in mind that Fatherhood does too, at least when we are referring to your Heavenly Father. He has kept this world running because of steadfast love and infinite patience. He must be as weary as most of His children are at the craziness that goes on in this world, but because He wants more people to be saved, He waits with patience and compassion.

As you look at your life today, you probably have a lot of reasons that your patience could be wearing thin. It may be your children, it may be your job, or it may be some other factors, but when you're growing weary of the things that cause you to feel that way, look up. Look up to your Heavenly Father and thank Him for having such infinite patience, the kind that continues to sustain the earth and keep it spinning on its axis, the kind that gives each of us a chance to have a better day tomorrow. As one of God's favorite people, dearly loved as the woman you are, give Him thanks and praise for His compassion and kindness and endless patience. May He calm your spirit and give you peace in all you must do, for by patience you possess your soul.

POSITIVE THOUGHTS WHEN YOU NEED PATIENCE

Think:
Peace, prayer, and a positive spirit.
Attitude adjustment.
Thankfulness.
Insights into someone's motives.
Ease into the moment.
No negative thoughts.
Compassion works.
Experience grace and love.

K. Moore

A GOOD REMINDER

Be as patient with others as God has been with you.

Author Unknown

AN APPLE A DAY

When God ripens apples He isn't in a hurry, and He doesn't make noise.

Sidney D. Jackman

INSPIRED THOUGHTS

Rest in the Lord; wait patiently for Him. In Hebrew, "Be silent in God, and let Him moule thee." Keep still, and He will moule [mold] thee to the right shape.

Martin Luther

TURNING TO THE BIBLE

Everything that was written in the past was written to teach us. The Scriptures give us **patience** and encouragement so that we can have hope.

Romans 15:4 NCV

TEACH YOUR CHILDREN WELL

To endure is the first thing that a child ought to learn, and that which he will have the most need to know. Jean-Jacques Rousseau

MOMISM

If I've told you once, I've told you a million times!

Mom's Prayer and Blessing

Dear Lord, I have much to learn when it comes to having patience. I'm often surprised at how little things can frustrate me. I don't like waiting in a line to get into the movies. I don't appreciate the person who has a pocketful of coupons when I'm trying to check out at the grocery store. It frustrates me when people are rude or when children are having a tantrum and a parent pays no attention. Being a mother, I've had to develop more skill in the area of patience, but I know I'm not there yet.

I pray that you will bless moms everywhere who are enduring any kind of hardship, whether it's unruly children, or circumstances that leave them uncertain about what life will be like down the road. Help me to be more patient with others so that I can shine Your light. I am better these days at handling frustrating situations because of You. You have changed me. I am better, but I look to You for strength and compassion and love. Help me develop the kind of patience with my family and with others that You always have toward me.

Amen

Work

Mom Needed: Low-Income/High-Stress Job

She does her work with energy, and her arms are strong. She knows that what she makes is good. Her lamp burns long into the night.

Proverbs 31:17–18 NCV

It would be difficult for advertisers to entice anyone into taking the job of mom based on the job description. After all, it would have to read something like, "Patient, kind, energetic woman who loves children even when they are difficult, needed for long-term care, with no time off and low salary." Of course, this description isn't far off from the Proverbs 31 woman who had strong arms, lots of energy and kept the candle burning long into the night. Perhaps the work of moms hasn't really changed much over the years.

You may not hear this often enough, but it's important for you to know that you've done a great job as a mom. You've blessed your family with your conscientious stick-to-it-ness and energetic demeanor. You've embraced the motherhood role with gusto and you've created a home where peace and smiles prevail. It wasn't an easy assignment, but you gave it all you got right from the start and you've continued on that path ever since. Bravo, Mom!

The work of being a mom may change over time as children grow into stable and healthy adults, but the influence and respect you've garnered will never go away no matter what age your children might be. You've been their rock, their foundation, the arms that comforted them and the voice that soothed them. You've watched over them from the moment they were born and so you shall all the days of your life. You've done an amazing job.

You've always taken your work as a mom to heart, as though you weren't just working for your family, but for a greater good, a bigger cause, as in working for the Lord. Perhaps the adage is true that "God could not be everywhere, and so He created mothers." He wanted someone in every home who would bless each person who lived there, equipping them with skills and talents that would serve them later on in life. You were chosen to be His hands and feet and His heart of love. God knows that, for you, the job will never be really over, never be totally accomplished because your heart and mind will follow your children wherever they go, praying for them and blessing them all the days of their lives. Thank you for the work you've done in building a great home and family.

MOM'S CREED

For anything worth having, one must pay the price;
And the price is always work, patience, love, and self-sacrifice.

John Burroughs

MOM'S WORK

Every mom is a working mom!   Author unknown

MOM'S LIFE

I never notice what has been done.
I only see what remains to be done.

Madame Curie

MOM'S ADVICE

Nothing is particularly hard if you divide it into small jobs.

Henry Ford

MOM'S ATTITUDE

I long to accomplish a great and noble task, but it is my chief duty to accomplish small tasks as if they were great and noble.

Helen Keller

MOM'S PERSEVERANCE

Diamonds are nothing more than chunks of coal that stuck to their jobs.   Malcolm S. Forbes

GIFTS FOR OUR CHILDREN

There are two lasting bequests we can give our children:
One is roots. The other is wings.   Hodding Carter Jr.

PRAYING MOMS

Praying moms are the soul support of their children.

Author unknown

WHAT MOM KNOWS

We can't form our children on our own concepts;
We must take them and love them as God gives them to us.

Johann Wolfgang von Goethe

MOMISM

A mother's work is never done!

Mom's Prayer and Blessing

Dear Father in Heaven, You already know that the work of a mother has its moments that feel confusing and difficult. There are times when I am uncertain about the advice I gave or the direction I suggested. I have my children's best interests at heart, but I can't know them quite the way You do. You know what they are about and what they are meant to become. You gave them to me to care for and love and I've done my best to embrace them in every way possible.

I never want to be out of a job when it comes to being a mother, because I really believe it represents some of my best work in the world. I look forward to seeing the people that my children will become as they step out on their own and begin to look to You for direction. Bless mothers all over the globe who struggle to raise their children with joy and kindness, keeping them safe and healthy, so they can grow up to be strong and responsible adults. It's a once-in-a-lifetime job, Lord, and I'm grateful for the chance to do it.

Amen

Wisdom

Moms Are Smarter than Anything!

*Teach us to number our days, that we may gain a heart of **wisdom**.*

Psalm 90:12 NIV

It's interesting to note that the writer of Proverbs metaphorically referred to wisdom as an enlightened woman. It says: "In her right hand, Wisdom holds a long life, and in her left hand are wealth and honor. Wisdom makes life pleasant and leads us safely along. Wisdom is a life-giving tree, the source of happiness for all who hold on to her."

You are smarter than anything! You are the one who takes note of everyone's schedule: doctor appointments, practices after school, and tests coming up. You know when the kids need to be shuttled from one place to another, and when they need time just to tell stories and be listened to. You are their source for good and for guidance and for all the things that make life work as they imagine it should. You are the one who knows what happened to their homework, which kid likes what kind of sandwich for lunch, and how to make the best brownies. You're an outstanding mom, even on days you don't feel like you have it all together.

Even wisdom needs a rest now and then. You try hard to make your family life pleasant, cheering on the home team, laughing at the silly things that happen, and watching out for the welfare of each person. Your understanding and insight are truly a life-giving tree, and everyone depends on you for love and steadfast support. You nurture your children to become their best selves and you give God the glory for all He has done.

Thank you for making every day count. Remember in your wisdom to also take care of yourself so that you can be strong and have peace of mind and heart. Those are the things that God offers you every time you spend a few moments with Him in prayer. He will replenish your energy, lighten your load, and hold fast to you to help you through every single day. With His help, you will keep growing in wisdom and then be ready to serve Him in the world. May you discover the richness of His love in all you do today.

GETTING WISER ALL THE TIME

If you realize you aren't so wise today as you thought you were yesterday, you're wiser today.

Olin Miller

A WISE WOMAN

A wise woman does not grieve for the things she doesn't have. She rejoices in the things she does have.

Adapted from Epictetus

THIS IS SO LIKE MOM!

Those who have the largest hearts have the soundest understandings.

William Hazlitt

WHAT MOM ALREADY KNOWS

Knowledge speaks; wisdom listens!

Adapted from Oliver Wendell Holmes

MOM'S HELPFUL FRIENDS

The next best thing to being wise oneself is to live in a circle of those who are.

C. S. Lewis

THE WISDOM OF CHRIST

She is truly wise who looks upon all earthly things as folly that she may gain Christ.

Adapted from Thomas à Kempis

IF YOU NEED ANOTHER DOSE OF WISDOM

But if any of you needs wisdom, you should ask God for it. He is generous to everyone and will give you wisdom without criticizing you.

James 1:5 NCV

WISE MOMS HAVE SECOND THOUGHTS

Among mortals, second thoughts are the wisest! Euripides

FAMILY WISDOM

We can't choose our relatives, but we can choose our thoughts, which influence us much more. Author unknown

MOMISM

A penny saved is a penny earned!

Mom's Prayer and Blessing

Dear Lord, You've been so gracious to me, inspiring my heart and mind as I care for my family. I do pray for wisdom because I have so many decisions to make all the time and I'm not always sure what the best course might be. You go before us and so You already know what I should do, and I trust You then to guide my steps as I work to support and nurture my family.

I don't often hear of people who ask You for greater wisdom, but I think it's one of the best things I can do. When Solomon was going to rule the nation of Israel, that's the one thing he asked of You. He wanted more wisdom because he didn't know if he could handle the needs of all those people without it. I have just a handful of people to care for in my house, Lord, but I still need wisdom to do it well. I pray that You will continue to walk with me and teach me the ways that I can be more perceptive, knowledgeable, and wise so that I can be the best possible influence and guide for my family. I thank You for watching over us each day. Amen

Action

Seeing Mom in Action

*Every good **action** and every perfect gift is from God. These good gifts come down from the Creator of the sun, moon, and stars, who does not change like their shifting shadows.*   James 1:17 NCV

No matter what age and stage your kids might be in, you've learned a lot about organizing your day and getting things done. You've had to manage everything from your own job, to household chores, to getting kids to school on time, and so your best defensive technique was to be prepared. You learned as your kids were growing up that there was always one more crisis that had to be handled, or one more tidbit of information that needed to be addressed at the last minute, and so you became flexible. You became a woman in continual action, moving through the to-do list, accomplishing your work goals, making meals, and staying up late to get it all done. There aren't too many superheroes who accomplish much more than you do during the day.

So what are the best action steps you can take to help yourself with all these tasks? What one thing can you do that will make a difference with all the other responsibilities you've taken on? You need your own guide, your own helping hand, so your first action step should be to sit down. That's right! Sit down and be still. Invite God to spend time with you and let Him know all the things that you have to do. Unload your to-do list and then cast some of your burdens on Him. After you've done all that, sit some more and listen. Listen for His voice and His thoughts about what you can do, what action you can take that will most bless your day and give you some relief as well.

Once you've set your priorities together, go back and review your list and determine which ones you can simply let go of, and which ones must be done immediately. Being a go-getter and take-action person doesn't have to be exhausting. You can be renewed and strengthened and fortified when you invite God in so that you are never working alone. God is your safety net, and He's always right there with you, ready to catch you and keep you securely in His hands. Rest in His presence at the start of each day.

AS THE DAY HEATS UP

Lord, grant that the fire in my heart may melt the lead in my feet.

Author unknown

LITTLE THINGS MEAN A LOT

Love's secret is always to be doing things for God, and not to mind because they are such very little ones. F. W. Faber

ADVICE FOR ACTIVE MOMS

Stop worrying about whether or not you're effective.
Worry about what is possible for you to do, which is always greater than you imagine. Archbishop Óscar Romero

MOMS HAVE A DIVINE PURPOSE

There is not a spider hanging on the wall that doesn't have an errand; there is not a weed growing in the corner of the church lot that doesn't have a purpose; there is not a single insect fluttering in the breeze that does not accomplish some divine decree.

And I will never believe that God created anyone, especially any Christian, to be a blank, and to be a nothing.

C. H. Spurgeon

KEEP GOING!

Never let what you can't do interfere with what you can do!

Coach John Wooden

NO NEED FOR COMPARISONS

Each person should judge his own actions and not compare himself with others. Then he can be proud for what he himself has done. Galatians 6:4 NCV

MOM'S HOUSEHOLD

Since you cannot do good to all, you are to pay special regard to those who, by the accidents of time, or place, or circumstances, are brought into closer connection with you.   Saint Augustine

MOMISM

Actions speak louder than words!

Mom's Prayer and Blessing

Dear Lord, You know how busy I am, that I am action oriented. I don't sit still very long, but it is not always easy to keep up with the responsibilities I have. You blessed me with work that I love, and a family to care for, and a great home. All I need is the strength to do everything those jobs require.

So I've come to You for help because You know me so well. You know the action steps I should take to manage the expectations of everyone who depends on me. You know what I need to perform all my jobs well. I pray for stamina to keep up with everything.

As a woman and a mom, let me remember to come to You as the Source of my strength so that I can please You and care for my family. Let me not take any actions that I have not stopped to pray about. I know that I can depend on You each day. Please bless moms everywhere who have too much to handle and give them help at the right time. Bless children all over the world.   Amen

Courage

There's a Superhero Inside Every Mom

*Take **courage** as you fulfill your duties; and may the Lord be with those who do what is right.*   2 Chronicles 19:11 NLT

Nobody would argue that it takes courage to be a parent, and even more so to be a mom. From the time a child is born, the expectations of a mom are high. Not only is she the one who willingly went through labor and delivery, she's the one who is there each day after that to offer comfort and nourishment and love. As far as a baby is concerned, mom is a superhero.

We love superheroes because they always show up in the nick of time. They know exactly what to do to defeat the enemies and they never have a thought for themselves. They simply jump in and get the job done. Now, doesn't that sound like what a great mom does?

You are a brave woman. You're committed to being the best mom you can be and you know that even when your children are fully grown, you won't feel that your job is done. You will still be there, showing up in the nick of time to offer comfort and advice and love. That's what you do. Your example is what helps your children grow, strengthening their understanding of life and giving them "people" skills. You are the teacher and the spiritual coach and the prayer warrior and the gourmet chef. You are the one everybody turns to when things are a bit crazy and they desperately need a hero, or perhaps some sweet peace.

If we look in your closet, we might not find a red cape that transforms you from a woman to Wonder Mom, but chances are good that you're the first one there when any child of yours calls and needs help. You inspire your family and friends because they see that God's Spirit is alive and well inside you. You light up the world anyplace you happen to be. Everyone loves a good hero, and in your family, that would be you. When the job is a bit overwhelming, though, the good news is that you can put your cape away and simply sit with God. He will renew your energy, inspire your heart, and keep you strong. May God continue to bless you and give you the courage you need each day to protect and love and nurture your children.

COURAGE FACES FEAR

Courage is fear that has said its prayers.   Dorothy Bernard

MOM'S MOTTO

I can do all things through Christ Who gives me strength.

Philippians 4:13 NIV

THE STAMP OF COURAGE

Courage is the first of human qualities because it is the quality which guarantees all the others.   Winston Churchill

HEROES

Heroes are not braver than anyone else, they are just braver five minutes longer than anyone else.   Ralph Waldo Emerson

MOM'S COURAGE AND FAITH

As I stood at the table, and just before I opened my mouth, the words of God came forcibly to my mind.

"Only be strong and of good courage."   Lord Shaftesbury

MOMS HAVE GREAT RESOLVE

Most of our obstacles would melt away if instead of cowering before them, we should make up our minds to walk boldly through them.

Orison Swett Marden

MOMS HAVE THE COURAGE TO WAIT

Wait patiently for the LORD. Be brave and courageous.
Yes, wait patiently for the LORD.   Psalm 27:14 NLT

BRAVE MOMS

Courage is what it takes to stand up and speak;
Courage is also what it takes to sit down and listen.

Winston Churchill

MOMISM

Money does not grow on trees!

Mom's Prayer and Blessing

Dear Father in Heaven, You're the only Superhero that I will ever meet. After all, You can do anything, see everywhere, be everywhere, and You never even get winded. It's amazing to think of all that You've done as the Creator of the universe, and everything else that goes way beyond the solar·system I live in. You even had the courage to create human beings, hoping that we would learn to love You and have a relationship with You. You brought us into being and yet You wait patiently for us to realize that You are there.

Thank You for my family and the children who have blessed my life. Thank You for giving me the strength to make hard decisions and the love to sustain them through all the things that prove difficult. Thank You for seeing each person on this planet as Your beloved child. Help me to grow in strength, doing all I can to follow Christ and live by His example. I praise You and thank You for my life, my family, and the gifts of happiness I've known from Your generous spirit. Amen

Truth

Mom Is the Sleuth of Truth

*But when the Spirit of **truth** comes, he will lead you into all truth. He will not speak his own words, but he will speak only what he hears, and he will tell you what is to come.*   John 16:13 NCV

Chances are that you recall a time or two as you were growing up when your mom asked a usual mom question like, "Where have you been?" or "What are you doing?" and you fabricated a little story. You weren't sure how she'd feel about you being at a party that wasn't chaperoned, or what she'd say if she knew you were smoking a cigarette. After all, these were things she already told you were bad for you. The problem with those little lies was that one way or another, Mom found out the truth, and then you were in for whatever favorite disciplinary measures she liked the most.

No matter what age you happen to be, it appears that most of us struggle with telling the truth, that is, the complete and utter truth. For good reasons and perhaps for protective reasons, we simply brush the truth aside and make up a good story that sounds plausible. After all, we don't want to hurt anyone's feelings.

As a mom, you probably recognize those moments when you're being told a story, over the ones where the truth is unveiled. After all, the older your kids get, the better you become at discerning reality from their short flight into fantasy.

So what does that mean in your spiritual life today? The reminder is simply that God is truth! That means He cannot lie to you ever. That means He knows what the truth is about you all the time, and therefore, when life is getting you down, you don't have to hide anything from Him. He knows everything already. The best thing you can do then is come clean and tell the whole truth. The quicker truth is on the table, the greater your position is to receive forgiveness and move on with your life.

This dynamic works between you and God because of Jesus, who died for the sins of everyone and cleaned up the mess of humanity. God washed us clean so we could spend eternity at His house.

Truth may be difficult, but lies can ruin your life. Each time you forgive your children, remember how often God has forgiven you. That's the kind of truth that will set you free. That's the kind of truth that will fill your heart with love.

PEEKING AT TRUTH

A tiny tot of two or three,
Created clever artistry,
But seeing mom come down the hall,
She said, "Who colored on the wall?"
When Johnny was a boy of eight,
He saw a cake upon a plate,
He quickly finished every crumb,
And said, "See what the dog has done."
From tots to teens, up through adult
We seldom feel ourselves at fault,
We look God squarely in the eye
And weave a tale, a little lie.
The problem is God always knows
The truth and how the story goes,
So just come clean right from the start,
And God will free your guilty heart.

K. Moore

STANDING FOR TRUTH

People will occasionally stumble over the truth, but most times they will pick themselves up and carry on.   Winston Churchill

MOM ALREADY KNOWS THIS

If a million people believe a foolish thing, it is still a foolish thing.

Anatole France

SEARCHING FOR TRUTH

Let us rejoice in the truth, wherever we find its lamp burning.

Albert Schweitzer

KNOWING THE TRUTH

"Then you will know the truth, and the truth will make you free."

John 8:32 NCV

MOMISM

If you tell a lie, your nose will grow!

Mom's Prayer and Blessing

Dear Lord, You forgive those places in our hearts where we deceive ourselves. You allow us to come to You and spread our deepest, darkest hurts and lies and leave them at the cross. There, You wipe them clean and give us the opportunity to change and grow and become more acquainted with Your truth. I pray for all of us who seek to be honest with You. Grant us grace and mercy as we struggle to tell You the stories You already know about us. Move our lies far away and open the doors of truth so that we have expanded hearts, ready to receive Your continual love.

Thank you for being the One to whom I can bare my soul. I pray for each person in my family to come to know You today.

Amen

The Lord Is Mom's Shepherd

The LORD is my shepherd;
I have everything I need.
He lets me rest in green pastures.
He leads me to calm water.
He gives me new strength.
He leads me on paths that are right for the good of his name.
Even if I walk through a very dark valley, I will not be afraid,
   because you are with me.
Your rod and your shepherd's staff comfort me.
You prepare a meal for me in front of my enemies.
You pour oil of blessing on my head; you fill my cup to
   overflowing.
Surely your goodness and love will be with me all my life, and
   I will live in the house of the LORD forever.

Psalm 23 NCV

Guide

Moms Embrace the Guidebook

*You keep your loving promise and lead the people you have saved. With your strength you will **guide** them to your holy place.*

Exodus 15:13 NCV

If you could create a handbook for your kids that contained your most inspired thoughts, some "how-tos" as they are going out on their own, and even a few of your favorite recipes, it would be a cherished manual for the rest of their lives. They could look up all the ways you taught them how to do things, and the advice you gave them for a variety of situations. They could look up the social etiquette guidelines you shared, and the nutritional menus you provided. They might see the best ways to organize closets or freeze certain leftovers. No doubt it would be one of the handiest guidebooks they could ever have, at least as far a mom guidebook goes.

The truth is they do have a guidebook and so do you. It was written centuries ago and is one of the most useful tools available anywhere. It gives the history of God's people, and it shares the wisdom of some of the great kings like David and Solomon. It has love stories and mysteries, miracles and battles. It offers hope when you feel uncertain and encouragement when nothing seems to be going your way. This guidebook intrigues readers because it is a living document. That means the words may be centuries old, but the reader gets an opportunity for guidance and direction that is meaningful right now. God put His Spirit into this guidebook in such a way that each reader can get exactly what is needed for their personal life situation.

The most important message in this book is the story of God's plan for our personal salvation, the story of the birth and death and resurrection of His only Son, Jesus. It's an amazing story and one that is worth reading over and over again, because that story affects your whole life. As a mom, you have a lot to deal with. Life can make you anxious and frustrated. It can make you grateful and delighted. Whatever is happening, the more time you spend in the Holy Bible, God's guidebook, the better you will manage all the situations you face in a day.

As you go into a new week, make sure you spend time with your favorite Guide and get inspired for all that you must do. There are more good tips for living a happy life in that book than any other book you could read. It's a great Word, and it's all for you!

GOOD TO KNOW

Where God guides, He provides.   Germany Kent

MOM'S FLASHLIGHT

And I said to the man who stood at the gate of the year: "Give me a light, that I might tread safely into the unknown."

And he replied, "Go out into the darkness and put your hand into the hand of God. That shall be to you better than light, and safer than a known way."   Minnie Louise Haskins

THE BEST GUIDE

Hang this question up in your houses—"What would Jesus do?" and then think of another—"How would Jesus do it?"

For what Jesus would do, and how he would do it, may always stand as the best guide to us.   C. H. Spurgeon

THE LAMPLIGHT

Thy word is a lamp unto my feet, and a light unto my path.

Psalm 119: 105 KJV

GOING MY WAY?

The strength and happiness of a person consists in finding out the way in which God is going and going that way too.

Henry Ward Beecher

SURRENDER TO YOUR GUIDE

As soon as we lay ourselves entirely at His feet, we have enough
light given to us to guide our own steps.　　　　　George Eliot

MOM'S POINT OF VIEW

Life becomes harder for us when we live for others, but it also
becomes richer and happier.　　　　　Albert Schweitzer

MOMISM

So it's raining? You're not sugar—you won't melt!

Mom's Prayer and Blessing

*Dear Lord, I thank You for being my faithful guide. I know that I have
often walked on without You, not waiting for Your guidance, and then
found myself in difficulty I didn't anticipate. I've not always listened to
Your advice, but stubbornly imagined I had all the answers.*

*It grieves me to know that I can do those things and at the same time
be unhappy when my children treat me the same way. Sometimes they
go off on their own and don't ask for guidance and sometimes they are
just stubborn. Remind me that as You work with me, so I need to work
with my children, forgiving them and shining a light on the path that
seems best.*

*Be with me, Lord, as I try to follow You, and bless my children as
they learn more about You as well, and as they try to listen to me. Your
grace and mercy fill me with hope every single day.*　　　　　Amen

Forgive

I Can't Believe I Did That!

*Yes, if you **forgive** others for their sins, your Father in heaven will also forgive you for your sins.*   Matthew 6:14 NCV

Wouldn't it be awesome if everything about you became, well, perfect, on the day you became a mom? You know, from the day you brought your first tiny infant home from the hospital, you discovered that you simply didn't make any mistakes. You followed all the rules, and if you weren't a living, breathing human being, God might simply nominate you for saint-hood. Alas, as great a mom as you are, you may still find that mistakes happen. Poor choices don't all just disappear, and angry words spill over into the air. You realize that not only do you need to be able to forgive others, and to forgive yourself, but every now and then others need to forgive you. Fortunately, you always get once-and-for-all-forgiveness from your Father in Heaven, anytime you turn your foolishness over to Him.

Sometimes your children need your forgiveness. The quicker you are at being the first one to offer forgiveness, the sooner the atmosphere becomes peaceful again.

The important thing to remember is that forgiveness is about love and it's about relationship. As one writer put it, "Forgiveness does not mean the cancellation of all consequences of wrongdoing. It means the refusal on God's part to let our guilty past affect His relationship with us." In other words, God forgives us so that we can come back to Him again and so we can all make up and love each other completely.

Moms do the same thing. You give your child a chance to be redeemed, to come back to your loving embrace and to recognize even foolish things can be repaired, with the power of forgiveness. Forgiveness is a love thing and one of the greatest gifts God gives to any of His children.

Keep in mind that God is always there for you, waiting to heal those things that trouble your heart, and ready to redeem you with His love!

WHEN WE NEED SOME MENDING

Forgiveness is the answer to the child's dream of a miracle by which what is broken is made whole again, and what is soiled is made clean.

Dag Hammarskjöld

MARTIN LUTHER'S DREAM

In a dream Martin Luther once had, he saw a book where all his sins were written.

In the dream, the devil spoke to Luther, "Martin, here is one of your sins, here is another," pointing to the writing in the book.

Then Luther said to the devil, "Take a pen and write, 'The blood of Jesus Christ, God's Son, cleanses us from all sin.'"

SEVENTY TIMES SEVEN

Then Peter came to Jesus and asked, "Lord, how many times shall I forgive my brother or sister who sins against me? Up to seven times?"

Jesus answered, "I tell you, not seven times, but seventy-seven times."

Matthew 18:21–22 NIV

A VIOLET FOR MOM

Forgiveness is the fragrance the violet sheds on the heel that has crushed it.

Mark Twain

A FORGIVENESS PRAYER

Dear Lord and Father of mankind,
Forgive our foolish ways!
Reclothe us in our rightful mind,
In purer lives thy service find,
In deeper reverence, praise.

John Greenleaf Whittier

AN ATTITUDE OF FORGIVENESS

Forgiveness is not an occasional act, it is an attitude!

Martin Luther King Jr.

MOMISM

Love means you always have to say you're sorry!

Mom's Prayer and Blessing

Dear Father, I know that I can't undo the past, or change those parts of my history that grieve my heart now that I know You better. But I trust that You can, and I believe that You have allowed me to be washed clean, and enabled me to move on, creating opportunities that help me grow and understand even more about the power of Your love. You cast my foolishness far away and help me to do better next time.

I'm so grateful for Your love and for Your forgiving heart. Lord, help me to have that kind of heart for my family and friends when things happen that offend me or grieve me. Help me to remember all You've done for me so that I can be more compassionate to others. Walk with me and with my children all the days of our lives so that we may know more of what it means to build a bond of deep love and reverence and joy in our relationship. Thank You for redeeming my sins so long ago and blessing my life.

Amen

Compassion

All Dressed Up and Ready to Go!

*Therefore, as God's chosen people, holy and dearly loved, clothe yourselves with **compassion**, kindness, humility, gentleness and patience. Bear with each other and forgive one another if any of you has a grievance against someone. Forgive as the Lord forgave you. And over all these virtues put on love, which binds them all together in perfect unity.*

Colossians 3:12–14 NIV

You probably have some favorite accessories. You have the sparkly blue earrings that go perfectly with your brilliant jewel-toned scarf. You have the shoes that match at least three of your favorite outfits. When you are called to dress things up a bit, you can go out with the best of them.

Perhaps you never really considered this, but God calls you to dress up each day for Him. He wants you to sparkle and shine for His kingdom in all the best ways. His idea of a great outfit is one that you can wear with compassion, kindness, humility, and gentleness. This outfit travels well, never gets wrinkled, and is ready at a moment's notice. It is so special that others notice it every time you wear it because it makes you so beautiful.

When you go through life as a woman of compassion, with a heart for God, then you see others with the eyes of your heart—you see them for what they can be, and not necessarily what they are at the moment. You actually see them as God sees them. This wonderful trait in you is one that helps your children and others to know that you are a loving and caring person. It shines as an example of what it means to be a woman of God. Your patience and forgiveness, your kindness and humility, inspire them to try harder, and to want to do better next time.

If you don't feel that you've been wearing this outfit much lately, ask God to help you be more of what He has called you to be. It's certain that the next time you check your closet, you'll be able to clothe yourself in ways that please Him.

MOM'S HEART

The dew of compassion is a tear.   Lord Byron

SHOWING YOU CARE

Anyone can criticize. It takes a true believer to be compassionate.
No greater burden can be borne by an individual than to know no
one cares or understands.   Arthur H. Stainback

GOD'S COMPASSION

The Lord is full of compassion and mercy.   James 5:11 NIV

MOM'S EMOTIONS

God has not created us to be like sticks and stones.
He gave us five senses and a heart of flesh so that we can love our
friends, be angry with our enemies, and have compassion on our
dear friends in adversity.   Adapted from Martin Luther

WHAT MOMS KNOW

To ease another's heartache is to forget one's own.

                    Abraham Lincoln

SOMETIMES WE CRY

Heaven knows that we need never be ashamed of our tears, for they
are rain upon the blinding dust of earth, overlying our hard hearts.

                    Charles Dickens

GOD DRIES OUR TEARS

The tearful praying Christian whose distressed heart prevents his
words, is clearly understood by the Most High.

                    C. H. Spurgeon

MOMISM

Treat others the way you want to be treated!

Mom's Prayer and Blessing

Dear Lord, You amaze me! You see us for what we really are, bear with our sins and our faults and yet continue with us, investing Your love and time in us so that we can realize how much we need You, so we can return to You. You are the God of my heart, and Your Spirit often reminds me to see the world heart first.

When I look at others, seeing You within them, I realize I feel connected to them, and want to do what I can to encourage them if they seem disheartened by life, or to inspire them if they have somehow lost their way. You have dressed me in compassion, and though I don't always understand what I can give, I know that I always desire to do something.

You have given me great compassion in raising my children and in helping them to grow in awareness of You and of the gifts and talents you've given them. Help me to be patient and kind with each member of my household first, and then to others as I step out into the world. Thank You for the example of what it means to embrace all that is tender about life. I am awed by your compassion for us, your wayward children.

Amen

Example

Mom Is the CEO

*Follow my example, as I follow the **example** of Christ.*

1 Corinthians 11:1 NCV

Moms have a lot of big jobs. Some work all day away from home and then come back to manage their own household, running errands, cleaning, making meals, reading stories, playing games. They watch over everything that involves their family and do all they can to keep things running smoothly. Basically, they are the CEO of the house...as in the Chief Everything Officer!

CEO moms know that they can't do their job alone, though. No matter how helpful the family members may be, the mom job needs some supernatural intervention. When you signed up to follow Jesus, you decided that He would be your life example, the One you would use as a standard for any of the work you do. When you have a doubt about what to do or which direction to turn, you pray. Your prayer is some version of asking Jesus what He would do or what He would guide you to do. That system works well because Jesus is *your* CEO.

You are a great example to others, but often, you need a good example that helps you remember why you make the choices you make. Jesus told stories in parables, using illustrations and examples from His day to help His followers understand more clearly the messages He had for them. Stories are good ways to remember important points, and you probably use that technique in your own family. Maybe you tell your kids stories about the way you learned certain things as a child.

Good examples are great teachers, whether they come from a person you follow, or a wonderful story that illustrates a point. You look for examples in Scripture or other books that inspire your heart and mind. When you're not quite sure what to do next, do more research. That's what a good CEO does because then they can confidently lead the way for others.

Example   75

It's always your day to be the example of what it means to follow the Leader, your personal guide!

A GUIDANCE MEASURE

A pint of example is worth a gallon of advice.   Author unknown

A GOOD EXAMPLE

An example illustrates a point
That serves to guide the way,
To strengthen each tomorrow
And bless your life today.   K. Moore

THE IMPORTANCE OF A GREAT EXAMPLE

Setting an example is not the main means of influencing others. It is the only means.   Albert Einstein

TURNING UP THE LIGHT

As we let our light shine, we unconsciously give other people permission to do the same.   Nelson Mandela

LEAD THE WAY

It is not fair to ask of others what you are unwilling to do yourself.
                        Eleanor Roosevelt

A MOTHER'S VOICE

Let us preach you, Dear Jesus, without preaching...not by words, but by our example...by the casting force, the sympathetic influence of what we do, the evident fullness of the love our hearts bear to you. Amen.   Mother Teresa

FOLLOW YOUR HEART

In every way be an example of doing good deeds. When you teach, do it with honesty and seriousness.   Titus 2:7 NCV

ONE MORE EXAMPLE

If doing a good act in public will excite others to do more good, then..."Let your light shine to all..."

Miss no opportunity to do good.

John Wesley

MOMISM

Because I'm the mother!

Mom's Prayer and Blessing

Dear Father in Heaven, You have so generously provided great examples for me to follow. You have given us countless stories from the Bible that illustrate the ways You would have us think and act toward others. You gave us Jesus, who is the ultimate example of obedience and love and sacrifice. I pray that I am a good example to my family, modeling the behaviors You would find pleasing and honoring You in the process.

Help me, Lord, to be the kind of example that is worthy, instructive, and honest. Let me be a light in the way I live my life that, even if I don't say a word, others come to know and understand more of who You are and how You would have us live. Bless my home and my family, giving each of us strength and opportunity to both be examples for good in the lives of others, and recognize when we need to follow more of Your example in what we do. Let me be the kind of mom that is always willing to carry Your light wherever I go.

Amen

Example 77

Thankful

Thanks for Giving Me My Crazy and Wonderful Family!

*Keep your roots deep in him and have your lives built on him. Be strong in the faith, just as you were taught, and always be **thankful**.*

Colossians 2:7 NCV

If you're like most moms, you have days when simply running away from your family might seem like a great option. After all, they can be a bit crazy and you really could use a nice quiet spot to simply sip some lemonade and read a good book. It's a great idea, but you are generally too busy for that little fantasy to take place.

You might also wonder from time to time how a nice woman like you ended up in the family you have. That is not a thought that questions your love for each member of your household, just one that reflects on the idealistic kinds of things that you imagine must be going on in other people's houses. Surely, everyone there picks up their own socks and puts their dishes in the dishwasher after they have made a snack.

The blessing to you, though, is that God knew what He was doing when He put you in the midst of the exact family you have. He knew they needed you to help them sort through the ups and downs of daily living. He knew they needed you to remind them of schedules and practices and other important things. You're the exact mom that fits with your crazy and wonderful family.

God also knew that you are a woman with a grateful heart, the kind that sees the gift in each thing He does to provide for your life. You are thankful when things turn out well, and prayerful when they don't. Your gratitude is a measure of the trust you place in God and He holds on to that trust, respecting all you do and embracing you each day. God loves a thankful heart and He knows all that You need. Give God thanks and praise for all He has done today. He loves your family and you in every way.

THANKFUL FOR LITTLE THINGS

Be on the lookout for mercies. The more we look for them, the more of them we will see...

Better to lose count while naming your blessings than to lose your blessings to count your troubles.   Maltbie D. Babcock

GRATEFUL FOR EACH DAY

In ordinary life we hardly realize that we receive a great deal more than we give, and that it is only with gratitude that life becomes rich.   Dietrich Bonhoeffer

A HEART OF GRATITUDE

Would you know who is the greatest saint in the world? It is not the one who prays most or fasts most.

It is not the one who lives most, but it is the one who is always thankful to God, who receives everything as an instance of God's goodness and has a heart always ready to praise God for it.

William Law

THANKS BE TO GOD

Both gratitude for God's past and current mercies, as well as hope-filled expectation of His future mercy, are the strongest motives to live for His glory.   Scott Meadows

MOM'S GRATITUDE

When you truly thank the Lord for every blessing sent,
Little time will then remain for murmurs or lament.

Hannah More

THANKFUL THOUGHTS

Let the peace that Christ gives control your thinking, because you were all called together in one body to have peace. Always be thankful.   Colossians 3:15 NCV

You'll thank me for this someday!

Mom's Prayer and Blessing

Dear Lord, I trust that You already know how grateful I am for my family. They are the joy of my heart and the gift to each day. Help me to take care of them in the best ways that I can. If we don't agree with each other, help us to be willing to hear each other out with compassion and mercy. When we are worried about something, help us talk to each other and then come before You and share our concerns.

Help me to be a mother who is wise in ways that bless each person I love. Give me insight and kindness as I offer advice or share my thoughts with them. Thank You for our home and for giving us the opportunity to work out life together. Nothing else I do gives me the kind of joy that comes from watching my family grow together in love. Thank You, too, for our extended family and friends, the people who so often support us with grace and compassion. I pray that You will strengthen us and renew us each day and help all of us to serve You with love.   Amen

Faith

Every Mom Is a Woman of Faith!

Now faith is confidence in what we hope for and assurance about what we do not see. This is what the ancients were commended for.

Hebrews 11:1 NIV

You've always been a smart woman and a perceptive and reasonable person. You apply both faith and reason to all the things you do as a mom. You handle things well when you can understand them or are able to reason things out for yourself. Other times, though, you have to go on faith. John Donne said, "Reason is our soul's left hand, faith her right."

When we understand the whys and the wherefores of things, we are more comfortable. Once you look at all the facts surrounding something that isn't quite clear, you feel better. After all, God gave you the gift of being able to reason, even offering at times that you could go to Him and the two of you could "reason" things out together.

Looking back at Donne's quote, though, it appears that reason could be the weaker hand to play. If the right hand is faith and it's a dominant hand, then it's the stronger player, the better ally. When reason fails, faith comes to the rescue. Faith intervenes and takes you where you need to go.

As you've already learned, raising kids isn't always a reasonable task. In fact, there are many times when you may feel clueless to understand what is going on when a circumstance arises. You may not be able to even guess what your child is thinking, much less how to reason it out.

The best thing you can do, then, is keep feeding your faith. Start your day with a prayer breakfast, feast on the Word for lunch, and refresh and nourish your heart and mind at dinnertime, knowing God has all things in His hand. Feeding your faith means you are starving your fears. Keep faith at your right hand and then raise your hand to God anytime you need an extra portion of His love and mercy. God sees you and He draws near to you every time you call His Name!

THE HANDLES OF FAITH

Every tomorrow has two handles. We can take hold of it by the handle of anxiety or the handle of faith.   Henry Ward Beecher

JUST A LITTLE FAITH CAN HELP

When we have an atom of faith in our hearts, we can see God's face, gentle, serene, and approving.   John Calvin

MOM'S FAITH AND LOVE

Say to yourself, "I am loved by God more than I can either conceive or understand."

Let this fill all your soul and never leave you. You will see that this is the way to find God.   Henri de Tourville

EVEN MOMS HAVE CHILDLIKE FAITH

A simple, childlike faith is a Divine Friend and solves all the problems that come to us by land or sea.   Helen Keller

GOD CHOSE YOU

Faith is from God, not from you. You can do nothing to earn or receive it. You are right with God by faith alone.   Martin Luther

FAITH WITHOUT "IFS"

Faith takes God without any ifs.
If God says anything, faith says, "I believe it," and faith says, "Amen" to it.   D. L. Moody

FAITH CARRIES YOU

A living faith is not something you have to carry, but something that carries you.   J. H. Oldham

LET FAITH LIGHT THE WAY

When you get to the end of all the light you know and it's time to step into the darkness of the unknown, faith is knowing that one of two things will happen.

Either you will be given something solid to stand on, or you will be taught to fly.

Edward Teller

BELIEVING IS SEEING

We live by faith, not by sight.

2 Corinthians 5:7 NIV

MOMISM

Red sky at night, sailor's delight!

Mom's Prayer and Blessing

Dear Lord, You know that I am a woman of faith, but I must admit that there are times when I just feel like I have to take matters into my own hands. I run in, clean up a mess, and then when things settle down again, I take the problems to You. For some reason, I always imagine that I should do what I can do before I bother You with what I can't do.

I pray that You would help me know when I should turn to You so that I don't spend needless hours worrying or simply wondering what steps to take next. I pray that my faith would strengthen me and that You would guide me in every circumstance and situation I face. I know that, on my own, I may not get it right or even understand that there's a good lesson I could learn from what is going on. Be with me and my family as we work through things that trouble us, and as we celebrate good things that happen too. Whatever direction my life takes, Lord, I come to You in faith, trusting You are always there and that I can draw near to You for answers to my needs, and for love and mercy for each day.

Amen

Persevere

Hold on to God's Promises

*You need to **persevere** so that when you have done the will of God, you will receive what he has promised.* Hebrews 10:36 NIV

If there's one thing that all moms have in common, it's "stick-to-it-ness." Moms know that the only way things will work out well is if they stick to the job at hand. You know, because you do it too.

When something doesn't work quite right, you look for a solution. When one of your kids has some kind of struggle going on, you stay with them until you figure out the answer. You know that the only way around something is to work your way through it. You do that as a mom, as an employee, and as a woman with dreams of her own. When you persist, insist, and keep moving forward, things happen. The one thing you must watch is that you resist any temptation to give up.

One way to stay the course and keep moving forward is to trust that you are not going through any difficulty you may have alone. You have a Source of love and light and possibility that you can plug into anytime you choose. God has promised to be with you. He also promises that if you cast your burdens on Him, He will carry them for you. He doesn't want you to carry them at all. He wants you to lay every struggle, every burden, every uncomfortable thought you have, right at His feet. Set them down and He will lighten the load. That is His promise!

You can get through the struggles when you are willing to stay the course, persevere, stick to your part of things, and let God do the rest. He will show up! He will help you. He has promised to be with you every step of the way. May you feel His presence today in all you do.

KEEP MOVING

In the confrontation between the stream and the rock, the stream always wins, not through strength, but by perseverance.

H. Jackson Brown Jr.

THE HEART OF PERSEVERANCE

Perseverance is the sister of patience, the daughter of constancy, the friend of peace, the cementer of friendships, the bond of harmony and the bulwark of holiness.   Bernard of Clairvaux

MOM'S CREED

All things are possible to one who believes,
yet more to one who hopes,
more still to one who loves,
and most of all, to one who practices
and perseveres in these three virtues.

Adapted from Brother Lawrence

REMEMBER THE TORTOISE

Slow and steady wins the race.   Aesop

THE MESSAGE OF PERSISTENCE

Nothing in the world can take the place of persistence.

Talent will not; nothing is more common than unsuccessful individuals with talent. Genius will not; unrewarded genius is almost a proverb. Education will not; the world is full of educated derelicts.

Persistence and determination alone are omnipotent.

Calvin Coolidge

CHEERING YOU ON

Be of good cheer! Do not think of today's failures, but of the success that may come tomorrow. You have set yourselves a difficult task, but you will succeed if you persevere; and you will find joy in overcoming obstacles.

Remember, no effort that we make to attain something beautiful
is ever lost.

Helen Keller

WE ARE WINNERS!

We are hard pressed on every side, but not crushed; perplexed, but
not in despair; persecuted, but not abandoned; struck down, but
not destroyed.

2 Corinthians 4:8–9 NIV

MOMISM

If you don't succeed, try, try again!

Mom's Prayer and Blessing

*Dear Lord, You know that I signed up as a mom for the long haul, not
for the short run. I know that too, but some days, I wonder if I will finish
the race. On those days, the challenges of parenting are beyond my
ability to either understand or control. I am certain that things will work
themselves out, but I come to You when I need a way to keep holding on.*

*You have given me a remarkable family and the opportunity to shine
Your light over each person. When my own light feels weak, though, I
wonder how to make it brighter. I pray that You will pour more of Your
Spirit into my tired and weary body and help to strengthen my resolve,
my hope, and my sense of peace.*

*Things are not always this way, of course. In fact, most of the time,
our lives run smoothly, and I know that You are the One who holds us up
and keeps us moving forward so positively. When it isn't going well, I'm
grateful that I can turn to You for strength to keep me persevering and
faithful to all that You have called me to do in my home and family.*

Amen

Think

One Good Thought Deserves Another

Fix your thoughts on what is true, and honorable, and right, and pure, and lovely, and admirable. **Think** *about things that are excellent and worthy of praise.*   Philippians 4:8 NLT

Moms are great thinkers! At night, after the work is done, they reflect on their day as they prepare the household to go off to dreamland. They think about tomorrow and what events have been planned that might be fun or interesting. They think about whether they could have said something differently or whether they shouldn't have said anything at all. After all, raising a family means that moms are involved in a lot of other people's cares and concerns all day long.

You're a thoughtful mother and a woman who thinks about the kind of difference you hope to make in the lives of people you love. You hope to influence those around you with love and kindness, inspiring their thoughts to want to try harder or do something better than they did before. You're continually looking for new ways to please your family and friends. You do this because you also want to please God. You want to be a great example of His love. You need to stay close to Him so that you can understand more of the ways He wants you to think and act.

To keep holding everyone else up, you have to watch what you think. You have to be careful about what you allow to go into your mind and concentrate your efforts and ideas around the things that are positive and right. The more you consider the good things—the ones that motivate you to keep doing all the things you do—the more you will shine for your family and for your Father in Heaven. He placed you in the family you have, and He wants you to hold on to the things that help you grow strong and feel loved. Shut off the news, step away from negative conversations, and say your prayers. God is with you!

The Scripture in Philippians is a great reminder of all the things you can think about that will fill your spirit with joy and serve to strengthen your heart and mind as a mom and as a friend. Remember, too, you are an excellent mom who is truly worthy of praise, so hold that thought today.

THINKING AND BELIEVING

A Christian is a person who thinks in believing, and who believes in thinking.

Saint Augustine

THINK WITH YOUR HEART

A person may think their own ways are right, but the LORD weighs the heart.

Proverbs 21:2 NIV

RENEW YOUR MIND, MOM!

Do not conform to the pattern of this world, but be transformed by the renewing of your mind. Then you will be able to test and approve what God's will is—his good, pleasing and perfect will.

Romans 12:2 NIV

CHANGE YOUR THOUGHTS

Change your thoughts and you change your world.

Norman Vincent Peale

MOMS BELIEVE IN THE IMPOSSIBLE!

"I'm just one hundred and one, five months and a day."

"I can't believe that!" said Alice.

"Can't you?" the Queen said in a pitying tone. "Try again: draw a long breath and shut your eyes."

Alice laughed. "There's no use trying," she said: "one *can't* believe impossible things."

"I daresay you haven't had much practice," said the Queen. "When I was your age, I always did it for half-an-hour a day. Why, sometimes I've believed as many as six impossible things before breakfast."

Louis Carroll, *Through the Looking Glass*

You've got another think coming!

Mom's Prayer and Blessing

Dear God, I thank You for providing us with so many wonderful things to think about. I rise each morning and think about how nice it was to sleep in a cozy bed and to enjoy the moments of quiet before the whole household is awake. I watch the sunrise and see the majesty of Your creation as it spills out over the landscape and brightens up the new day.

Remind me, Lord, when my heart is heavy that I have many things that are beautiful and inspiring to consider. I think about the delightful ways that You have influenced my heart and mind and have changed me into being the person I am today. I think about each of my children and the members of my family and rejoice in our similarities and celebrate our differences. Only You could have created each of us to be exactly as we are. Thank You for giving me endless reasons to hold positive thoughts, lavishing Your love on my family and filling us with peace and joy. Watch over each person I love today and guard the thoughts of their hearts wherever they may go. Amen

Integrity

Setting the Bar for Honesty

*"As for you, if you walk before me in integrity of heart and uprightness…
and do all I command and observe my decrees and laws, I will establish
your royal throne over Israel forever."*   1 Kings 9:4–5 NIV

As a mom, you do your best to be honest with your family and with yourself. You work to be fair and generous to those around you. You like people
who are straight shooters and so you try to be that way too. In fact, telling
the truth is one of your unspoken house rules. You just assume each person will do so because everyone wants to walk with integrity. Or do they?

It appears that God was concerned that the leaders of His people would
be honest and follow His guidelines. He wanted them to obey His house
rules because He was working on carving out the people He would call
His own. He wanted them to live by His standards. As you know, when
you review the stories of Israel's kings, honesty was seldom the case. In
fact, most of the rulers were without integrity or moral fiber of any sort.
They made life miserable for everyone.

Perhaps one of the reasons God is so interested in people who are
honest is because it is a rare thing. In fact, dishonesty got those garden
dwellers, Adam and Eve, into great trouble. That lying snake in the grass
disrupted their lives so much they had to give up paradise.

Doesn't that happen to us too? When we lie to those we love, we give
up the beautiful relationship we have, and live in fear of being discovered.
We fear the truth will come out and cause our conscience to go haywire.
We have a Jiminy Cricket moment and wonder if we'll end up with Pinoc-
chio's nose.

When your three-year-old can look you right in the face, just after
drawing a bright red line on your white wall, and say she didn't do it, you
can see how difficult integrity is.

The good news is that your family has you. You are an example of what it means to be honest, and you help them do better the next time when they've crossed the line. All you must remember is that God graciously forgives even our dishonest mistakes if we're willing to seek His face. Now that's the truth! May His grace and mercy be yours as well.

BE TRUE TO YOURSELF

This above all: to thine own self be true,
and it must follow, as the night the day,
thou canst not then be false to any man.   William Shakespeare

POPULARITY CONTEST

Truth is not always popular, but it is always right.

Author unknown

BE A BLESSING

Good people who live honest lives will be a blessing to their children.   Proverbs 20:7 NCV

GIVE INTEGRITY A CHANCE

Integrity: define it, deliver it, delight in it; create a place where it can be seen in everything you do.   K. Moore

A BIT OF WISDOM

Truth is the first chapter in the book of wisdom.

Thomas Jefferson

AN HONEST THOUGHT

Our lives improve only when we take chances—and the first and most difficult risk we can take is to be honest with ourselves.

Walter Anderson

MOMS SERVE WITH INTEGRITY

To give real service you must add something which cannot be bought or measured with money, and that is sincerity and integrity.

Donald A. Adams

Honesty is the best policy!

Mom's Prayer and Blessing

Dear Lord, I do my best to be honest with others and to live my life with integrity. It's important to me to be able to hold my head up high as a Christian woman, as a mom, and as Your servant. I admit there are times when I have fallen into the trap of telling someone I had an appointment when I didn't want to get together or saying I thought an outfit was "stunning" even though it wasn't my taste at all. I guess I see those things as an effort to not really say how I feel, but I know they are not exactly honest.

Whatever else I do, help me to be as honest with my friends and family as I possibly can and, more than that, to be totally honest with You. Thank You for keeping me honest as You listen to my frustrations and my plans. You help me to face good news or even disappointment with integrity. I praise You and thank You for drawing near to me today and for causing me to desire to be an honest woman. Amen

Heart

Nobody Has a Heart Like Mom

*Above all else, guard your **heart**, for everything you do flows from it.*

Proverbs 4:23 NIV

You've always been a good-hearted person, and since the day you were born, you've been learning what it means to follow your heart. You know that it's important to protect your heart because it is the place where all your choices are made.

Jesus told us to seek God and love Him with "all your heart, all your soul, all your mind, and all your strength." When you start there, it is likely that you will be so filled with love that it will spill out to all those around you. Think about that little word "all." If you love God with all your heart, that means it's used up, there's nothing left; you've dedicated every bit of breath and life and strength to God. You have put God in the center of your life so that He can help you with everything else you do.

It's not easy to understand what it means to love with all your heart until you think about your children. Suddenly the picture clears up and it looks possible because you know that you have dedicated your life to loving the people you brought into the world. You love them with your whole heart.

The strength that you have then comes from your wholehearted love of God, and your genuine love of your family. When you have days where you've lost heart or you simply don't feel loved enough in return, then you always have a place to go. You can put everything else aside and seek God's strength and compassion. He will guide you back to where you feel safe and strong again.

One of the reasons your family loves you so much is because they can't imagine anyone who could love them more than you do. You are their example of what it means to love with your whole heart. You help them understand more than anyone else ever could what it means to love God as well. You make God smile!

AN OPEN HEART

Neither prayer, nor praise, nor the hearing of the Word will be profitable to those who have left their hearts behind them.

C. H. Spurgeon

MOM'S LOVE

Who listens when you're feeling blue,
Who says, "There's no one quite like you,"
Who loves the silly things you do?
Mom!
Who makes sure your homework's done
And then suggests, "It's time for fun."
And brings a smile to everyone?
Mom!
Yes, God made Moms to help Him care
For His children everywhere,
And that's why no one can compare...
With Mom!

K. Moore

KEEP SMILING

A happy heart makes the face cheerful, but heartache crushes the spirit.

Proverbs 15:13 NIV

HEART STRINGS

The best families are tied together with heart strings.

K. Moore

MOMISM

Nobody loves you like I do!

Mom's Prayer and Blessing

Dear God of my heart, You have blessed me beyond measure and in countless ways. I praise You for the abundance and joy I have received. I know that You have watched over my family and You have provided our daily bread and much-needed support. You forgive us when we fall short of being the people we can be, and You strive to keep us from making unwise choices. You have been so good to us.

I pray that my heart would grow so that I am filled to the brim with You, so I can be more considerate and loving to my family. I pray that You would strengthen me when I feel uncertain or confused. Remind me that You are always near, and protect my heart from those things that could cause me to fall. Watch over the hearts of each person I love, providing the armor of Your Spirit and grace. When life is difficult, help us to work our way through whatever remarkable circumstances we face and rest in Your mercy. Thank You for loving us so much.   Amen

God's Promises

You: It's impossible!
God: **All things are possible with me.**
You: I'm too tired!
God: **I will give you rest.**
You: Nobody really loves me.
God: **I love you.**
You: I can't do anything more.
God: **My grace is sufficient for you.**
You: I can't forgive myself.
God: **I forgive you.**
You: I'm afraid!
God: **I have not given you a spirit of fear.**
You: I'm just so worried and frustrated!
God: **Cast all your burdens on Me.**
You: I'm not smart enough!
God: **I give you wisdom.**
You: I feel all alone.
God: **I will never leave you nor forsake you.**

Family

All in Mom's Family

Whoever does not care for his own relatives, especially his own family members, has turned against the faith and is worse than someone who does not believe in God.   1 Timothy 5:8 NCV

The definition of family has grown to mean everything from those who are your biological relatives to those who are your dearest friends in the world. However you define it, there is nothing that means quite as much as knowing you have people in your life who stick with you through the good times and the bad. They stand by you when you act a little bit crazy, and they continue to love you no matter what else is going on. Your family ties are important, and they help sustain you your whole life. After all, these are the people who have to take you in when you knock on the door.

Moms generally set the tone in a family. When they are generous and positive, joyful and loving, everyone thrives. When they are troubled, clouds hang over the whole household. God put you in a family because He knew they would be good for you and you would be good for them. You have each other to lean on no matter what comes your way, and you have God's love too.

Because God is your Father, you are part of His family, and part of His community of believers. When difficulties arise, these are the family members you can turn to for help. Billy Graham said that "the family was ordained by God before He established any other institution, even before He established the church."

Where else can you show up and be yourself, burn the pot roast and they'll still eat it, or sing off-key in the choir and still be loved? Your family is your support system and your best opportunity to give and receive love. As a mom, you provide the gift of faithful love they all need. They simply couldn't do it without you. May God bless your family today.

FAMILY TIES

His name is the Lord—rejoice in his presence!
Father to the fatherless, defender of widows—
This is God, whose dwelling is holy. God places the lonely in
families.

Psalm 68:4–6 NIV

FAMILY EDUCATION

The mind of Christ is to be learned in the family. Strength of
character may be acquired at work, but beauty of character is
learned at home. There the affections are trained.

Henry Drummond

SUSTAINABLE FAMILIES

Family life is too intimate to be preserved by the spirit of justice. It
can be sustained by a spirit of love which goes beyond justice.

Reinhold Niebuhr

FAMILY DIFFERENCES

God is the first object of our love:
Its next office is to bear the defects of others.
And we should begin the practice of this amid our own
household.

John Wesley

RAISE UP A CHILD

The family should be a place where each new human being
can have an early atmosphere conducive to the development of
constructive creativity.

Edith Schaeffer

MOMISM

A little soap and water never killed anybody!

Mom's Prayer and Blessing

Dear Lord, I thank You for my remarkable family. They are the ones who sustain me and remind me of the important things in life. They hold me up and laugh with me, walk with me when I feel out of sorts, and give me room to try again when I fail. I've learned so much from being a mom and sometimes I wish I had learned faster, so that I could have done a better job right from the beginning. I'm grateful for our love for one another and for all that You have provided for us.

I pray that You would bless the families of our friends and of people who do not have the kind of friendship and support that we enjoy. Bless them with positive spirits, with financial help, and with compassion for each other. Help them to desire to know more of You so that they have You to turn to when things are not going well for them. I praise You for the gift of family. You have blessed me beyond measure! Amen

Friend

Mom Is a Faithful Friend

A friend is always loyal, and a brother is born to help in time of need.

Proverbs 17:17 NIV

Perhaps you remember that point in your relationship when your mom was no longer just the authority figure, or the guide, or the one who helped you understand the rules of life, but she was also a friend. You were able to have conversations about almost anything, sharing your thoughts with mutual respect and love. It may have seemed a bit awkward at first, but there was something very special about realizing you had grown up enough to be Mom's friend.

If it hasn't happened already, you will experience that kind of moment with your own kids. They will come to you for advice, and you will offer it, knowing that they can make up their own minds, and that they could move forward with or without you. The difference is that now they are grown up enough to realize how smart you really are and how much you know that they may not have the experience of knowing yet.

Being a friend to someone you raised is a unique kind of experience and fills your heart with joy. This kind of friendship and maturity is what your Father in Heaven wants too. He wants to talk with you as a friend, knowing you respect and love Him and trust Him to hear you out. You go to Him for advice, and to shine a light on your path. When you can do that with real joy, you know that you have developed confidence in God and that you accept Him as the One you can go to about anything that troubles you. You can count on His faithful and steadfast love, the same way your children count on you.

It's good to be a friend to your grown-up children, and it's better yet to grow strong enough in your relationship with God to feel that you have a friend in God, your Father.

May God bless your relationships with each dear person that you call friend.

YOU ARE MY FRIEND

[Jesus said:] "You are my friends if you obey me."   John 15:14 CEV

THE TIMING OF FRIENDSHIP

Sometimes being a friend is mastering the art of timing:

There is a time for silence, a time to let go and allow people to hurl themselves into their own destiny.

And a time to prepare to pick up the pieces when it's all over.

Octavia E. Butler

WALK WITH ME

Don't walk behind me, I may not lead.
Don't walk in front of me, I may not follow.
Just walk beside me and be my friend.   Albert Camus

TO BE A GOOD FRIEND

To have a good friend is one of the highest delights of life;
To be a good friend is one of the noblest and most difficult undertakings.   Author unknown

YOU, TOO?

Friendship is born at that moment when one person says to another: "What? You, too? I thought I was the only one."

C. S. Lewis

WHEN YOUR LIGHT GOES OUT

Sometimes our light goes out but is blown into flame by another human being. Each of us owes deepest thanks to those who have rekindled this light.   Albert Schweitzer

MOMISM

If you can't say something nice, don't say anything at all!

Mom's Prayer and Blessing

Dear Father in Heaven, I thank You for being a friend to me. You are there when I cry out to you in need, when my heart is heavy, or my concerns for others are too much for me to handle. You allow me to cast my burdens on your shoulders so that I can walk more easily, as You inspire my heart and soul.

Thank You, too, for my dear friends who sustain me when I need cheer, who walk with me when I don't want to walk alone, and who remember me always with love and joy. Thank You for the gift of Your friendship, which enriches my life and sustains my spirit.

Help me always to be the kind of friend I would like others to be to me. Give me patience and the ability to listen more than I speak; give me words of encouragement to share and give me a heart to serve You and the people I love most in the world.

Amen

Serve

Mom's Cooking Up Love!

*Each of you should use whatever gift you have received to **serve** others, as faithful stewards of God's grace in its various forms.*   1 Peter 4:10 NIV

Whether you are an awesome cook or simply skilled at coming up with just the right ways to plan dinner, your family is grateful for all that you do to serve them so well. Of course, they may not always show it, but you know it's true. You use every gift God has given you to put love on the table, even if it's from the local take-out place. Your wide variety of talents help make life run smoothly because you are the teacher, the referee, the counselor or the advisor, the listener, and the provider. Whatever role you play, you do it with all you've got.

You may not think about what you do for your family as a service to them because you do everything out of love. You do your best every day, and even when you're weary, you do your part to keep everybody happy. You may not feel exactly like the woman in Proverbs 31, who is able to make absolutely everything from scratch. It appears she's so talented she can plant a field, spin the yarn, run a business, and still manage her household without a hitch. You may be tempted to idolize her or wonder how you could ever keep up with a woman like that. You are not in a competition, though; you are the one person who keeps your family a priority. You do every task from washing the clothes to planning vacations, to creating birthday surprises, and you manage your household just fine.

If your family could sew, they'd present you with a red cape, adorned with a sparkly giant "M" on it, to celebrate what a hero you are to all of them. You are a faithful steward of all that God has given you, and because of that, He blesses your life and the lives of the people you hold dear. He sees your efforts and your willingness to serve them without question or complaint. He sees your heart and knows that you are motivated by love and your faithfulness to Him.

You're a great mom who uses all her God-given talents and skills to the fullest, so your family is truly blessed no matter what you are cooking up next. Bravo for you!

MOMS SERVE SO WELL

The greatest reward for serving others is the satisfaction found in your own heart.

E. C. McKenzie

MOM'S REWARD

No mom was ever honored for what she received. Honor has been the reward for what she gave.

Adapted from Calvin Coolidge

ODE TO MOM

It's Mom who wipes away the tears,
Brings the smiles, calms the fears.
It's Mom who shops and cleans and cooks,
And Mom who shares her love of books.
It's Mom who always does her part
To give her love, right from the heart!

K. Moore

MOM'S COMMITMENT

I won't have any money to leave behind. I won't have the fine and luxurious things of life to leave behind. But I just want to leave a committed life behind.

Martin Luther King Jr.

WHAT MOMS DO BEST

Do what you can with what you have where you are.

Theodore Roosevelt

NOTE TO MOM

We are all pencils in the hand of a writing God, who is sending love letters to the world.

Mother Teresa

WHAT MOM DOES

She speaks wise words and teaches others to be kind. She watches over her family and never wastes her time.

Proverbs 31:26–27 NCV

MOMISM

Fake it till you make it!

Mom's Prayer and Blessing

Dear Lord, You know I love doing things for my family. I love to make a great dinner and have everybody smile. I love to order pizza and know that it means we'll have a fun night to share. I enjoy anything that keeps everyone feeling good and keeps us all healthy and motivated to do the things we each have to do. Thank You for giving me this family and helping me serve them with love because it is one of the highlights of my life.

I feel honored that You chose to put me in this family, knowing what I could bring to them that would help them grow, and knowing what they would bring to me that would help me grow as well. It's a privilege to be a mom and I don't take my job lightly. I know that I need Your strength and Your guidance to help me do it well. Give me the right heart, the kind of wisdom that I need to bless each one, and the energy to keep doing what I do best. I pray that I will serve my family with gusto and that I will serve You with joy.

Amen

Time

Once Upon a Time, There Was a Great Mom!

*There is a **time** for everything, and everything on earth has its special season.*
                                    Ecclesiastes 3:1 NCV

As a mom, you have a story to tell. You write it a little bit each day, noting milestone achievements, building memories. Raising your kids from infants to adults is a special season in your life. It's a blessing and a challenge and an opportunity all rolled into one. It's the great story of a unique job that gives you significant influence over the people around you. You're the first glimpse of what it means to be loved, and the first one to teach life's basic rules. You are the best guide God could give, and everyone is pleased to be part of your story. It's a season, and for most moms, it's a season that passes too quickly.

Sure, there are days when you wonder if you'll ever accomplish the tasks of motherhood. Can you keep up with the schedules and the appointments and the practices after school? Can you inspire their thinking so that they will try harder on a bad day, and learn to celebrate the good days? You don't want the days to hurry by because they quickly become yesterdays and are gone. Today is your chance to nurture the hearts and minds of your children.

If these days have already passed for you and your children are fully grown, perhaps even parents themselves now, you still have an opportunity to share your love and your time and your stories of God's grace and mercy with them.

Whatever season you're in, make the most of it. Spend your time wisely and well so that you have nothing but amazing memories to carry into the future. If you missed out on a step here and there, take the time right now to reignite the flame of love you have for your family.

If physical or emotional distance has occurred, then keep sharing stories and heartfelt prayers. Seek God's guidance and Spirit to watch over and protect the people you love. Your family's "once upon a time" story is the best one ever written!

THE VALUE OF TIME

Be more careful of losing your time than you are about losing your money.

Place such value on time that you do not waste it, but actively pursue things that bring you joy and teach you how to live.

Let no one rob you of your time, because today is the day the Lord has made and He made it for you. Author unknown

NOW!

There is only one time that is important—NOW! It is the most important time because it is the only time we have any power over.

Leo Tolstoy

THE PRESENT MOMENT

The present moment holds infinite riches beyond your wildest dreams. Be present in your present!

Adapted from Jean-Pierre de Caussade

FOR TODAY

Look to this day...
Yesterday is but a dream, and tomorrow is only a vision:
And today, well-lived, makes Yesterday a dream of happiness, and every tomorrow a vision of hope. Kālidāsa

GOD'S TIMING

A thousand years in your sight are like a day that has just gone by, or like a watch in the night. Psalm 90:4 NIV

MOMISM

Okay! I'm counting to three!

Mom's Prayer and Blessing

Dear Lord, I must admit that I scarcely know where the time goes. I feel so often like I simply rise to the new day, check a few things off my to-do list, and then clean up the kitchen after dinner and go to bed, only to do the same thing all over again the next day.

I want to be more present each day in the things I do, and in my interactions with my family. When I'm talking to one of my children or even to a friend, I want to be listening intently, taking in what they want to share with me, and then offering my thoughts in return. Sometimes I'm distracted, and I listen with one ear, thinking about other things I need to do, nodding politely, and missing what was really being said. Forgive me for crowding out life this way.

I pray that I would spend more quality time with You and more time with the people I love every day. Thank You for giving me the opportunity to grow and learn and understand the things that are truly important. Thank You for helping me measure my time wisely. Amen

Laughter

Moms Need Lots of Laughter

When the LORD brought back his exiles to Jerusalem, it was like a dream!
*We were filled with **laughter**, and we sang for joy.*
And the other nations said, "What amazing things the LORD has done for
them."
Yes, the LORD has done amazing things for us! What joy!

Psalm 126:1–3 NLT

As a mom, you can't help but notice the amazing things God has done in your life and in the lives of your children. Sure, not everything has been easy, but everything has moved forward, changing, growing, and becoming stronger all the time. Whatever age and stage your kids are in now, you have been there for them, watching each step of their progress, doing what you can to make things possible so that opportunities and challenges could be met head-on.

One of the gifts that moms often bring to the table is the gift of laughter. They know when to lighten things up. They know when everybody needs a break, a pizza, or a visit to the ice cream parlor. Sometimes a little bit of silly, just plain fun, can change everyone's mood and make the day brighter. Now and then, you need to take a break with your friends, simply to tell stories and laugh and let life pass you by for just a little while. God blesses your laughter and your fun times and those moments when you are simply clearing your head. Getting a break helps you be a better mom—living, loving, laughing, and working hard to guide and protect your children.

If you haven't asked God for a time-out, an opportunity to share with friends to talk about life and love and the experiences of being a mom, then do so soon. Pray for a positive spirit that can keep the balance and the joy in all that you do because it will surely do you good. God loves to see you laugh!

YOUR BEST ACCESSORY

You're never fully dressed without a smile.   Author unknown

COMMUNICATION

Laughter is the shortest distance between two people.

Victor Borge

MOMS SHOULD JUST BE MERRY

Always laugh when you can; it is cheap medicine.
Merriment is a philosophy not well understood.
It is the sunny side of existence.   Lord Byron

THE EXERCISE OF LAUGHTER

Laughter is inner jogging.   Norman Cousins

WHAT LAUGHTER DOES FOR YOU

Laughter can relieve tension, soothe the pain of disappointment,
and strengthen the spirit for the formidable tasks that always lie
ahead.   Dwight D. Eisenhower

HEAVENLY LAUGHTER

If you're not allowed to laugh in heaven, I don't want to go there.

Martin Luther

GRATEFUL FOR LAUGHTER

Of all the things God created, I am often most grateful He created
laughter.   Charles Swindoll

WHEN SARAH LAUGHED

Sarah said, "God has brought me laughter, and everyone who hears
about this will laugh with me."   Genesis 21:6 NIV

MOMISM

We're laughing with you, not at you!

Mom's Prayer and Blessing

Dear Lord, You know how much I need a little more laughter in my day. Help me to remember that it's not only okay to laugh, but that it is good for my soul. Remind me to lighten up so that I can enjoy those things that You have given me with a positive spirit and a grateful heart.

Thank You for children, who give us plenty of opportunities for smiles and even for laughter, cheering the moment simply by their sweetness and the way they delight in the world. Remind me to look through the lens of my childlike faith so that I see all the good things that are intended for me.

I know that laughter is the best medicine and so I pray that I will be blessed with many reasons to experience healthy doses of laughter throughout the day. Bless the people in my family and those who need to be uplifted by a smile today, and bring them surprised delight. I pray that I will delight Your heart and even give you a reason to laugh with joy today. Amen

Humble

Mom Never Eats Humble Pie

*But those who exalt themselves will be humbled, and those who **humble**
themselves will be exalted.*   Matthew 23:12 NLT

Most moms are humble women. In part, they are unassuming because
they focus on their job of parenting. They do their best to lift everyone else
up and encourage their plans and dreams. Moms are like the set deco-
rators of a play—they make everything beautiful, but they mostly stay
behind the scenes. They get to set the scene and then see how it plays
out—and they are good with that.

In a way, that's what God does too. He created the world and put us in
our communities and our families and gave us a special place to be. He set
the scene and then He gave each of us a starring role. He watches to see
how well we will play our part. Sometimes you're the star, but your humility prevents you from really thinking about that. Other times, you're the
supporting actor because you are the encourager and the nurturer. You
make sure that everyone else can play their part well.

Often, you are also the director and producer of your show, running
the most important scenes by Your Creator. Thank God for choosing you
for the role you have and seek His help anytime you need more direction.
You can be sure that He is proud of your efforts. He knows your family
appreciates all you do, even if they seldom say so. You are a humble person, knowing what God has done to give you all that you have. You don't
have to eat humble pie because you've never thought life was just about
you, and so the role suits you perfectly. Your humble heart and generous
spirit serve your family well.

Take a bow for being the incredible heart of your family, a great mom,
and a woman of committed faith, strength, and humility. Bravo for you!

HUMBLE ROOTS

Humility is that holy place in which God bids us to make the sacrifice of ourselves.   Author unknown

A HUMBLE HEART

Without humility of heart, all the other virtues by which one runs toward God seem, and are, absolutely worthless.

Angela of Foligno

LIFE LESSON

Life is a long lesson in humility.   James M. Barrie

WHERE HUMILITY GROWS

Humility is a strange flower. It grows best in winter weather, and under storms of affliction.   Samuel Rutherford

HUMBLE PRAYERS

Let us pray much for humility, and especially for humility in our days of peace and success.   C. H. Spurgeon

MOM'S BLUE RIBBON OF VIRTUE

True humility—the highest virtue, the mother of them all.

Alfred, Lord Tennyson

BE HUMBLE

Humble yourselves before the Lord, and he will lift you up.

James 4:10 NIV

MOMISM

Be proud, but don't get a big head!

Mom's Prayer and Blessing

Dear Lord, I am so grateful to You for my life and for the blessings you have poured out onto my family. I am awed by Your willingness to bear my burdens and to lift me up when I am uncertain about where I stand or what I'm doing. I am grateful each day for the gifts I see in my children, ones that I can celebrate, blushing with humble pride as I see them accomplish something they've worked hard to master.

I pray that you will bless them throughout their lives as they learn to use their gifts wisely. I'm happy to be the woman behind the scenes, helping to set the stage for each member of my family so that they perform well wherever they are. I'm grateful that You have shown me where I can do more to help them, and how I can share my time with them in better ways.

Lord, I am humbled that You have walked with me and loved me and showered me with endless blessings. When I forget to give You the glory, please remind me to have a bite of humble pie. Amen

Worry

*Can any one of you by **worrying** add a single hour to your life?*

Matthew 6:27 NIV

Even if you weren't a person who worried much before you became a mom, it's likely that the day you brought home your first little bundle of joy, you activated your worry gene. At first, it was little worries about things like, "Am I feeding the baby enough? Am I holding the baby okay? What should I do when the baby cries?" Slowly, but surely, you discovered the answers to those questions, only to see that, with each age and stage, you had other reasons to worry. "Is this the best kindergarten?" "Should I move to another town to get into a better middle school?" "Are parents going to be present at the party I'm going to attend?"

No doubt, you could list endless things that crossed your mind, and chances are good that few of those worries ever provided answers or gave you peace of mind. The thing you worried about probably never came to fruition, and so before you knew it, you learned that worrying simply didn't do you any good.

The funny part is that even though you know that, and you recognize the truth in the Scripture above where Jesus comments that worry can't add a single hour to your life, you still haven't found the off switch. You still haven't figured out the cure for the worry gene.

So here you go, here's something to consider. Worry may well give you something to do, but it won't take you anywhere. Why not pray instead? Pray about every detail of the things you are concerned about. Pray, seek God's advice and protection, and wait to hear His voice. It's likely that prayer will bring about change...in you. It will remind you that God is with you, that He knows your situation and that He's in charge. Prayer will bring you peace so that worry doesn't take over like a wild weed and choke out your faith.

You've got all you need to overcome uncertainty, worry, and those little fears that give you an anxious heart. Trust that God knows everything you need, and put your burdens in His hands. He's got this! Trust Him! It's okay to give up worrying.

GIVE GOD YOUR WORRIES

Give all your worries and cares to God, for he cares about what happens to you.   1 Peter 5:7 NIV

COME BACK DOWN TO EARTH

If you believe that feeling badly or worrying long enough will change a past or future event, then you are residing on another planet with a different reality system.   William James

THINGS WILL WORK OUT

I believe God is managing affairs and that He doesn't need any advice from me. With God in charge, I believe everything will work out for the best in the end.

So, what is there to worry about?   Henry Ford

A LITTLE STORY FOR YOU

A man ninety years old was asked to what he attributed his longevity.

"I reckon," he said, with a twinkle in his eye, "It's because most nights I went to bed and slept when I should have sat up and worried."   Dorothea Kent

MARTIN LUTHER'S CHAT WITH BIRDS

"Good morning, theologians! You wake up and sing. But I, old fool, know less than you and worry about everything, instead of simply trusting in the Heavenly Father's care."   Martin Luther

PEACE FOR MOM, PLEASE!

Oh, how great peace and quietness would the person possess who should cut off all vain anxiety and place all confidence in God.

Thomas à Kempis

MOMISM

Call me when you get there so I know you're all right!

Mom's Prayer and Blessing

Dear God of Peace, I know that I can worry about the smallest things. Anxiety just comes running into my room the moment I wake up in the morning. It seems to follow me around and, for some reason, provokes my worst thoughts.

I know those rocking-horse worries just give me something to do, but they don't take me anywhere. Remind me, Lord, that I can get off the worry-go-round and find a quiet spot to pray. Draw near to me and listen to my fears, the big ones and the small ones, and let me know You are right there with me.

Grant me that peace that only You can give, the kind that is just way beyond my understanding and open my eyes to see Your hand at work in my life and in the lives of the people I love so much. I'm not really sure if there is a worry gene, but help me to stop worry in its tracks and keep my faith in Jesus. I can cast all my burdens on You and pray you will soothe my soul. Thank You for Your continual blessings and love. Amen

Listen

Moms Know When to Talk, and When to Listen

Let the wise listen and add to their learning, and let the discerning get guidance—

for understanding proverbs and parables, the sayings and riddles of the wise. Proverbs 1:5–6 NIV

It's probably not a surprise to most moms that kids seldom need a good "talking to" as much as they need a good "listening to." Everybody needs someone to hear their thoughts and pay attention to the things that concern them. Kids are great because, when they are young, they persist in asking questions so that you have to hear them and answer. They love to know that they have been heard.

You were once one of those kids and so you know what it means to you when your spouse or your good friends, or someone dear to you, will take the time to listen to you. You have a heart that wants to share and a voice that longs to be heard. Even moms who are more inclined to be reflective and quiet look for opportunities to share what they think and feel with the right person.

By now, you've learned that it helps to be a good listener for others if you want them to listen to you in return. As an active listener, you ask questions or give feedback so that the other person knows you understand what they are saying.

So how are your listening skills when it comes to your prayers? You're probably good at thanking God for your life and seeking advice for your needs, but how good are you at being still? How good are your listening skills when it comes to your one-on-one time with God?

The next time you start to pray, apply a five-minute rule where you get to talk with God for one minute, and He gets to talk to you for four minutes. See if that exercise improves the quality of your communication. God loves it when you talk to Him, but He also loves it when you stop everything else and focus attention just on Him, anxious to hear what He has to say, hanging on to every word, and asking questions when you don't fully understand. If you're going to spend time with your Creator, then give Him a chance to share those things that will guide you and give you peace. You may be surprised at the amazing things He has to say.

LISTEN TO THIS!

My dear brothers and sisters, always be willing to listen and slow to speak.

James 1:19 NCV

AN OLD SAW

We have two ears and one mouth so that we can listen twice as much as we speak.

Epictetus

LIKE WISE MOMS

A wise old owl sat in an oak,
The more he saw, the less he spoke.
The less he spoke, the more he heard,
Why can't we all be like that wise old bird?

English nursery rhyme

LISTENING TO GOD

God is our true Friend, who always gives us the counsel and comfort we need.

Our danger lies in resisting Him; so it is essential that we acquire the habit of hearkening to His voice, or keeping silence within, and listening so as to lose nothing of what He says to us.

We know well enough how to keep outward silence, and to hush our spoken words, but we know little of interior silence. It consists in hushing our idle, restless, wandering imagination, in quieting the promptings of our worldly minds, and in suppressing the crowd of unprofitable thoughts which excite and disturb the soul.

François Fénelon

LISTEN WELL

Wisdom is knowing when to speak your mind and when to mind your speech.   Farmer's Almanac

MOMISM

Do you have beans in your ears?

Mom's Prayer and Blessing

Dear Lord, I thank You for being so willing to draw close to me when I need to share my heart with You. You know how often I come running, needing to confess my mistakes in judgment or choices or looking to You for advice so that I do things better next time.

Lord, I pray that You would also help me to be a better listener. Help me to wait for You, to be patient in the waiting, and to embrace Your peace. Your loving Spirit touches my heart and soul and helps me to be calm. I know that You have important things to share with me and that I will receive more from You when I listen with all my heart.

Prayer is such a miraculous thing! I can't quite take it in that the One who created the whole universe and things way beyond my imagination is willing anytime to hear my feeble voice, and lift me up, and encourage my life. You are so awesome, God! I am beyond grateful for all that You have done!   Amen

Beauty

No One Is More Beautiful than Mom!

It is not fancy hair, gold jewelry, or fine clothes that should make you
beautiful. *No, your beauty should come from within you—the beauty of a*
gentle and quiet spirit that will never be destroyed and is very precious to
God. 1 Peter 3:3–4 NCV

Beauty may well reside in the eye of the beholder, but you can ask nearly any child in the world, and they would likely say that Mom is the most beautiful woman they have ever seen. That means, you are beautiful!

Women spend a good share of their lives being told what beauty is and what it looks like. We are bombarded with magazine ads that remind us that we'll never have an air-brushed face and no amount of makeup will cause us to look like the woman we see on the page. Unfortunately, the ads and the beauty experts have missed the point. True beauty isn't on the outside at all; it's on the inside. Your beauty is reflected in your soul and in your heart. Your beauty comes from that sacred place where God is cleansing and molding and shaping you to become more of what He called you to be.

The light that shines in your eyes and the smile that warms your face make everyone notice you, because you shine with God's light. You are so precious in His sight and He loves all that you do to embrace those around you. Your kind heart and gentle spirit are a breath of fresh air to those who live in almost perpetual shadows and hopelessness. You make a difference simply by being beautiful you.

Today is your day to put on your happy face, shine your tiara, and let the world know there's more to life than what they experience. All they have to do is keep washing away their sins, opening up their hearts, and letting everyone see the light of God's perfect love shine through their eyes. Have a great day and make it beautiful! May God bless you and keep you sparkling for Him!

CHARACTERISTIC BEAUTY

Characteristics which define beauty are wholeness, harmony, and radiance.

Thomas Aquinas

DEFINING BEAUTY

Ask the earth and the sea, the plains and the mountains, the sky and the clouds, the stars and the sun, the fish and animals, and all of them will say, "We are beautiful because God made us." This beauty is their testimony to God. Ask men and women, too, and they know that their beauty comes from God.

Yet what is it that sees the beauty? What is it that can be enraptured by the loveliness of God's creation?

It is the soul which appreciates beauty. Indeed, God made people's souls so that they could appreciate the beauty of His handiwork.

Saint Augustine

TRUTH AND BEAUTY

The pursuit of truth and beauty is a sphere of activity in which we are permitted to remain as children all our lives.

Albert Einstein

LOOKING FOR BEAUTY?

Though we travel the world over to find the beautiful, we must carry it with us or we find it not.

Ralph Waldo Emerson

DIVINE BEAUTY

The being of all things is derived from divine beauty.

Thomas Aquinas

WISDOM AND BEAUTY

My child, hold on to wisdom and good sense. Don't let them out of your sight.

They will give you life and beauty like a necklace around your neck.

Then you will go your way in safety, and you will not get hurt.

Proverbs 3:21–23 NCV

Pretty is as pretty does!

Mom's Prayer and Blessing

Dear Lord, I awaken every day to the beauty that surrounds me as the sunlight flows through the windows, and the blue sky beckons me to start again. You have brought us continual opportunities to witness Your glory and the magnificent landscapes You created all over the earth. It is awesome to behold.

I learned a long time ago that beauty is so much more than a pretty face. Beauty lights up the souls of those who reflect Your Spirit and shine Your light. Those who know You well are radiant with joy and compassion, and with hearts that seek ways to serve You.

Help me to be beautiful in Your eyes by doing more of the things You have designed me to do. Remind me that I am Your child and in Your hand I can't help but become more beautiful with each passing day. Thank You for all that You provide that causes me to desire to live in beauty. Amen

Life

Having the Time of Your Life

God loved the world so much that he gave his one and only Son so that whoever believes in him may not be lost, but have eternal life.

John 3:16 NCV

Through God's grace and blessing, you brought a new life into the world. You helped to create a tiny human being, someone unique, someone who would grow to become a child of God. It was a miracle moment, and whether that moment was a few months ago, or several years ago now, you will remember that day for the rest of your life. It was the day you became a mom!

When God breathed life into Adam, He watched over him, making sure that he had what he needed to live in a way that would bring him joy. After a time, God realized that Adam wasn't happy being alone, that he needed someone who was more like him so that he could share his thoughts and his heart. God brought Eve into the world so that Adam and Eve could share life together.

For all of us, sharing life with others is essential. We need people to love. You've learned a lot of life lessons by now, discovering things about yourself, looking for ways to share your heart. God wants to help you understand more clearly what it means for you to live abundantly. Certainly, answers vary, but many people would say that a rich, full life needs to have love, and laughter, and friends and family. Life needs to have purpose and significance, opportunities and challenges. For any of us to truly recognize the essence of life, we need a place to call home, and a place for our restless spirits to find peace.

Each day, you can have the time of your life, as you make the most of what God has given you in your dedication to your family and to your life on this planet.

May you feel the blessing of His divine grace as He watches over you, just as He did over Adam and Eve, seeking to discover more of what you need to make your life worthwhile. Give God the thanks and praise for all that you have and all that is yet to be in your abundant life. After all, He lives in your heart!

WHAT I WANT IN LIFE

I asked God for all things that I might enjoy life.
I was given life that I might enjoy all things.   Author unknown

LIFE'S ANSWERS

In the book of life, the answers aren't in the back.
                                        Charlie Brown (Charles Schulz)

LIFE AND LOVE

Life is not a holiday, but an education. And the one eternal lesson for us all is how better we can love.   .   Henry Drummond

WHAT EVERY MOM KNOWS

Life is one long process of getting tired.   Samuel Butler

A MEANING OF LIFE

The life of the individual only has meaning insofar as it aids in making the life of every living thing nobler and more beautiful.

Life is sacred, that is to say, it is the supreme value to which all other values are subordinate.   Albert Einstein

YOUR BEST LIFE

Order your soul; reduce your wants;
Live in charity; associate in Christian community;
Obey the laws; trust in Providence.   Saint Augustine

ABUNDANT LIFE

I have come that they may have life, and have it to the full.

John 10:10 NIV

MOMISM

You only get to go around once. Make the most of it!

Mom's Prayer and Blessing

Dear Life-Giver, You breathed life into my soul the day that I accepted Jesus. You offered me the breath of salvation, the eternal life that I could never have secured on my own. I thank You and praise Your Name for all You've done to make sure that I can come back home to You when this life is done.

Lord, there is no one like You. I know that each time a child is born, You see that new person and bless the days that they will walk on this earth. You don't ever forget who we are and You call each one of us by name. To me, that is life! That is knowing that whatever portion I have here, it is nothing compared to the life I will have with You in the future.

I am so blessed by all you've done for me. You've given me an awesome family and friends who have stuck with me in good times and difficult times. You've watched over us and brought us Your peace when we were overwhelmed. You help us to see Your hand at work in all that we do, and I am forever grateful. I pray that You will continue to bless my life, my family, and all those who look to You to live the most amazing life possible. Amen

Can You Help Me?

— ⚬ —

A weary mom was leaving work,
She'd had a busy day,
As she reached the elevator,
Her boss came up to say,
"I just sent you an email,
It's something that can't wait,
Can you look at it this evening
And get it back to me by 8?
Can you help me?"

She told him not to worry,
She'd be sure to get it done,
And as she opened her front door,
She ran into her son.
He said, "Mom, it's time for science fair,
And I sure want to win,
I need some great ideas,
Before I can begin,
Can you help me?"

She hustled toward the kitchen,
Not sure just what to make,
When her daughter came in hurriedly

And said, "We have to bake.
I need cupcakes for tomorrow,
But I forgot to let you know,
Can we do it after dinner,
Before my favorite show?
Can you help me?"

Then Mom said, "Do your homework,
Or head outside to play,
I need a minute to myself,
And off she went to pray.
She opened up her Bible
And as she began to read,
She felt the Lord draw near
And so she shared her every need,
Can You help me?

She said, "Father, I'm so tired,
It's been a busy day
And I don't know where to start
But I've come to you to pray."
And God said, "Rest a moment,
Let Me offer you a hand,
I will strengthen you and help you,
With all the things you've planned.
Yes, I'll help you!"

She ordered pizza for their dinner,
Baking cupcakes as they ate,
She shared ideas with her son
He really thought were great.
And once she tucked the kids in bed,
And frosted chocolate treats,

She found her boss's email,
Cleaning up a few spread sheets.

As she settled in her blankets,
She took a moment yet to pray
And with a grateful heart
Here's what she had to say.
She said, "Lord, I was so weary,
I couldn't think at all,
And then I heard a voice inside
Inviting me to call,
That said, 'I'll help you!'

"And the minute we connected,
You renewed my heart and soul
And helped me take on every task,
Since You were in control.
So remind me then tomorrow
When I go about my day
That I simply must remember
You're with me all the way.

"And no matter what I face,
Or what I have to do,
If I pray to You for strength,
You'll always see me through.
Because You help me!

"Thank You, Father . . . good night!
K. Moore

Acknowledgments

I'd like to dedicate this book to some of my favorite moms. Those would include my great-grandmother Jennie Crance, who gave me my first Bible; my mother, Beverly Moore, who taught me how to make a great apple pie; and my daughters, Rebecca Gurney and Stefanie Barbour, two of the most amazing moms I've ever known. My heart goes out to all the moms who make a difference in the lives of their children every day.

It's a privilege to be a mom, and the best moms embrace their children with a love that goes beyond weary days, busy schedules, and household chores. They are moms who guide with wisdom and patience, love with their whole hearts, and give kids a reason to smile. May God bless all moms with courage and the gift of laughter.

I'm grateful to my husband, Bruce Barbour, for inspiring the whole idea for the series of *What a Great Word* books and who inspires my life every day as he walks faithfully with God.

I thank Hachette Book Group and FaithWords, especially Rolf Zettersten and Keren Baltzer, for catching the vision for this series.

Finally, thank you to my personal editor, Joan Matthews, who did an amazing job. May God continue to bless the work of your hands.

What a Great Word for Moms Alphabetical List

About the Author

KAREN MOORE is the best-selling author of more than 100 books for kids, teens, and adults with her inspirational daily devotionals. Karen teaches at writing conferences and is a keynote speaker for conference events and women's groups. Karen has also worked in the greeting card industry, creating thousands of greeting cards, as a product development specialist, and she's also worked as a book publisher. Currently, Karen is working on two licensed properties for children. She is married and makes her home near Savannah, Georgia.